WELCOME TO

OKLAHOMA

Discover the Excellence.

D1591365

Alva
Ponca
Cimarron
Woodward
Enid
North
Shattuck
Perry
Seiling
Canadian
Guthrie
Watonga
Canadian
River
Clinton
El Reno
Elk City
River
Washita
Moore
Sayre
40
Chickasha
OKLAHOMA
29
BROADWAY MUSICAL
USA
OKLAHOMA!

Oklahoma
BACK ROAD RESTAURANT
Recipes

A Cookbook & Restaurant Guide

ANITA MUSGROVE

Great American
COOKBOOKS

GreatAmericanPublishers.com · 888-854-5954

Great American
COOKBOOKS

ISBN 978-1-934817-49-0

by Anita Musgrove

First Edition

10 9 8 7 6 5 4 3 2 1

Design & Layout: Nichole Stewart
Layout: Zak Simmons
Editorial Assistant: Heather Martin

Great American Publishers

171 Lone Pine Church Road • Lena, MS 39094
TOLL-FREE 1.888.854.5954 • www.GreatAmericanPublishers.com

Contents

Welcome to Oklahoma

Preface

Hello again, friends. Are you ready for an Oklahoma road trip? Fans and friends have traveled with me through Alabama, Kentucky, Louisiana, Missouri, North Carolina, South Carolina, Tennessee, and Texas. This ninth book in the series is guaranteed to be another awesome trip as we travel The Sooner State, enjoying the best foods Oklahoma's locally owned restaurants have to offer. Little Brown, my Mercury who faithfully took us through all the previous states, had to retire, so now we are traveling on new wheels.

My first trip to Oklahoma was in 1998, when my daughter, Sheila, asked if Leonard, my husband, and I could take her oldest son, Ryan, to a special eye doctor in Ardmore. Of course, I said yes, not only to help my daughter but also to visit Oklahoma. Never having been to the state, we were looking forward to the opportunity to travel some new back roads.

So off we went in the wee hours of the morning through Mississippi, Louisiana, and Texas before finally crossing into Oklahoma; sixteen hours in the car is a long trip for a young, energetic boy. Thanks to some new Matchbox cars, lots of snacks, and new places to see, the trip was a lot of fun, especially the last three hours of quiet time when Ryan grabbed a nap. No more "When are we going to stop?", "Where are we going to eat?", or "Can we stop for fireworks?"

WESTERN
NORTHEASTERN
CENTRAL
SOUTHEASTERN
HISTORIC
OKLAHOMA
US
66
ROUTE

When we made it to Ardmore, it was cold. We arrived to discover the electricity was out in the hotel. Then, hours before dawn, I heard this sweet little voice hollering, "Granny, get up! It is snowing!" I looked outside, and, sure enough, a sea of white flakes was floating gently to earth to join the three inches that had already accumulated overnight. Leonard did not like the cold, so guess who got to go play in the snow. And play we did while Leonard kept the car nice and warm.

Traveling the back roads can be an adventure, but the best part is finding great mom-and-pop restaurants to stop at along the way. To help you travel The Sooner State, we have separated Oklahoma into five regions. Let's begin our journey in the Southeastern Region and make a stop at **Debbie's Bus Station Café** in Seminole for some of the finest *Quick Biscuits* around. She shared her recipe on page 225, along with a delicious *Chicken Soup*. Also in this region is **Hochatown BBQ**, located in the heart of Beavers Bend State Park. The restaurant shared their recipe for *Hochatown BBQ Baked Beans* as well as the best way to make *Hochatown BBQ Brisket* on page 199.

Keep the car running because next we are headed to the Northeastern Region and the city of Bartlesville. In 1957, Bartlesville was the test site for paid cable television. Now it's home to **Painted Horse Bar & Grille**, where the owners believe in three essentials to operating a restaurant: a cool, old historic building, quality food and beverages, and great service staff. And Painted Horse has it all. Try their *Moscow Mule* recipe on page 57. In the Northeastern Region, you'll also discover **Trenchers Delicatessen**, a Tulsa favorite that takes pride in roasting and smoking their own deli meats as well as making their own bread, pastries, desserts, and even condiments. In short, they make it all. And it's all delicious.

Moving on to the Central Region of Oklahoma, we find **Granny's Kitchen**. Though the name has changed over the years, the restaurant's location, family, and flavors date back to 1945. You'll enjoy down-home dishes, the feeling of being home with family, and the welcoming feel of the Stillwater community. Stillwater is also home to the National Wrestling Hall of Fame and Museum. Don't forget to stop in Norman and eat at **Scratch Kitchen & Cocktails**. They are "nerds about flavor" and share their *Steak au Poivre* recipe on page 157.

As we travel the Western Region, let's visit **The Sugar Shak** in Medford, where we can enjoy the Big Daddy—a yummy pulled pork, ham, and pepper Jack sandwich on a toasted hoagie bun. No, they did not give me the recipe for the Big Daddy, but you'll find their recipes for *Chicken-Bacon-Ranch Nachos* and the *Chicken Fajita Wrap* on page 35. You just about have to be lost to find the **Backdoor Steakhouse** in Blair. So let's get lost and enjoy Backdoor's famous blooming onion or one of their succulent steaks.

If you follow the STATE BACK ROAD RESTAURANT RECIPES SERIES, you know I love sunrises and sunsets. I have seen both in Oklahoma, and they are truly amazing. I felt like I could see forever with few lights and fewer buildings to block the magnificent views that allow you to marvel at the grandeur of God's creation.

It takes a team to produce a best-selling cookbook series, and I am blessed to have the best team around. First, always, is my God, who is ever awesome and blesses me in more ways than I deserve. Leading our team are the owners of Great American Publishers—Roger and Sheila Simmons, who take a personal interest in our lives, including our spiritual lives by encouraging us daily to live right and keep Jesus in our hearts. From the moment a book starts to the day it goes to the printer and beyond, everyone in the company has a hand in it. It would take a whole book to say what all the people in our company mean to me, so I will keep it simple. Thank you to my production partners and office mates, Nichole, Zak, and Heather. To Brooke, Diane, Christy, Amber, Tasha, Teisha, Tory, and Kristen, I give a big thank-you from my heart to yours. In my personal life, I owe a great big,

heartfelt thank-you to Richard Shaw, my best friend and traveling partner who supports me on good days and bad, and Missy, who welcomes me with wags and kisses and warms my heart each time she curls up in my arms.

And thank you, all my readers. You are the best. This book would be nothing without you. May God keep you safe always. This isn't the end of our journey. I'm working now to bring you the best locally owned restaurants in Mississippi. For now, let's eat!

Anita Musgrove

Anita Musgrove
Author

Whether therefore ye eat, or drink, or whatsoever ye do, do all to the glory of God.

1 Corinthians 10:31

Western

BACK DOOR STEAKHOUSE
BLAIR, OKLAHOMA

400 South Zinn Avenue
Blair, OK 73526
580-563-2000

You've got to be lost to the find the award-winning Backdoor Steakhouse. The restaurant has proudly served southwestern Oklahoma for more than fifteen years. Guests can dine on succulent dishes made with prime USDA cuts, such as ribeye, filet mignon, New York strip, and prime rib. You must start your meal with Backdoor's famous blooming onion or one of their other delicious appetizers. The steakhouse also offers a full-service bar that boasts a selection of beer, liquor, and wine to pair with your meal. Make Backdoor Steakhouse your first stop in Blair.

Monday – Saturday: 5:00 pm to 10:00 pm

Hungarian Goulash

3 onions, chopped

2 carrots, chopped

2 green bell peppers, chopped

3 pounds stew meat

¾ teaspoon salt, divided

¾ teaspoon pepper, divided

2 tablespoons olive oil

1½ cups low-sodium beef stock

¼ cup all-purpose flour

3 tablespoons paprika

2 tablespoons tomato paste

1 teaspoon caraway seeds

1 clove garlic, minced

1 dash sugar

1 cup sour cream

12 cups uncooked whole-wheat egg noodles, prepared per package directions

In a 5-quart slow cooker, combine vegetables. Sprinkle meat with ½ teaspoon salt and ½ teaspoon pepper, then, working in batches, brown in olive oil in a large skillet over medium heat; transfer to slow cooker. Add stock to skillet, stirring to loosen browned bits; add all remaining ingredients except sour cream and noodles. Add remaining salt and pepper. Bring to a boil, stirring 2 minutes or until thickened. Pour sauce into slow cooker, cover and cook 7 to 9 hours on low setting or until meat is tender. Stir in sour cream and serve over noodles.

Family Favorite

Chicken-Zucchini Casserole

1 (6-ounce) package stuffing mix

¾ cup melted butter

3 cups diced zucchini

2 cups cooked cubed chicken breast

1 (10.5-ounce) can cream of chicken soup

1 carrot, shredded

½ cup chopped onion

½ cup sour cream

Preheat oven to 350°. In a large bowl, stir together stuffing mix and butter; scoop out ½ cup and reserve for topping. Add zucchini, chicken, soup, carrot, onion and sour cream to remaining stuffing mix. Stir well, then transfer to a greased 7x11-inch baking dish. Top with reserved ½ cup stuffing mixture. Bake, uncovered, 45 minutes or until golden brown and bubbling.

Family Favorite

Warren Café

21183 Highway 19
Blair, OK 73526
580-563-2706
www.warrencafe.wixsite.com/warrencafe
Find us on Facebook

Welcome to Warren Café, a Blair staple that is the perfect gathering place for good food, good friends, and good company. The café serves breakfast and lunch, so from morning to afternoon, they have all your hunger pangs covered. Enjoy eggs, bacon, sausage biscuits, pancakes, French toast, burgers, sandwiches, burritos, chicken strips, taco salad, onion rings, chili dogs, and so much more. Warren Café also features a kids' menu, so you can bring your little ones with you. After you dine, ask your waiter about the homemade fried pies— the perfect dessert. Come for the food; stay for the down-home hospitality.

Tuesday – Saturday: 7:00 am to 2:00 pm

Homemade Biscuits

2 cups all-purpose flour
1 tablespoon baking powder
1 teaspoon salt
1 tablespoon sugar
⅓ cup shortening
1 cup milk

Preheat oven to 425°. In a bowl, whisk together flour, baking powder, salt and sugar. Cut in shortening with a fork until mixture resembles coarse cornmeal. Slowly stir in milk. Turn out dough onto a clean, well-floured surface and knead 15 to 20 times. Roll out dough to 1-inch thickness; cut out biscuits with a large biscuit cutter. Brush off excess flour and arrange biscuits on an ungreased baking sheet. Bake 15 minutes.

Restaurant Recipe

Lila McComb's Fried Pies

1 stick butter (or ½ cup margarine)
½ cup milk
1 egg yolk, beaten
¼ teaspoon salt
2 cups flour
**Fruit pie filling of choice
(apple, strawberry, etc.)**

Preheat deep fryer to 350°. In a large bowl, mix together all ingredients except pie filling; roll out dough to ⅛-inch thickness and cut into 6-inch circles. Add 1 to 2 tablespoons pie filling to center of each circle. Dampen edges with water, fold over into semicircles and seal quickly, crimping edges with a fork. Fry pies in deep fryer 5 to 8 minutes or until crust is golden brown.

Restaurant Recipe

Peanut Patties

2½ cups white sugar
3 cups shelled raw peanuts
⅔ cup Karo syrup
1 stick butter
1 tablespoon vanilla extract
1 cup milk
4 drops red food coloring
3 cups powdered sugar

In a saucepan over medium heat, combine white sugar, peanuts, Karo and ½ cup water; stir constantly until mixture reaches soft-ball stage (235° to 240°). Remove saucepan from heat and stir in remaining ingredients. Drop tablespoonfuls of mixture onto a baking sheet lined with wax paper, about 3 inches apart to accommodate spreading. Let cool before eating.

Restaurant Recipe

Cherokee Station Steakhouse

1720 South Grand Avenue
Cherokee, OK 73728
580-596-2882
Find us on Facebook

If you're looking for a unique meal or a family-oriented, hometown restaurant, look no further than Cherokee Station Steakhouse. The Station serves an array of delicious meats and seafood as well as the best cuts for your enjoyment. From buttery homemade yeast rolls to daily soup to the fresh salad bar, everything at Cherokee Station is made from scratch with the freshest produce and ingredients. The Station also serves Sunday brunch,

which features homemade desserts. Whether it's a company meal, dinner with friends, or a birthday dinner, the Station's expansive menu caters to each. The team at Cherokee Station Steakhouse invites you to join them for a savory meal.

Lunch:
Wednesday – Saturday: 11:30 am to 2:00 pm
Sunday Buffet: 11:45 am to 2:00 pm
Dinner:
Wednesday – Saturday: 5:30 pm to 9:00 pm

Sirloin Steak Sauerbraten

1½ pounds sirloin steak
1 tablespoon olive oil
1 (0.87-ounce) envelope brown gravy mix, prepared per package directions
1 tablespoon dried minced onion
1 tablespoon packed brown sugar
2 tablespoons wine vinegar
1 teaspoon Worcestershire sauce
¼ teaspoon ground ginger
1 bay leaf, crushed
½ teaspoon salt
½ teaspoon seasoned pepper

Preheat oven to 350°. Cut steak into cubes or strips. In a skillet over medium-high heat, brown steak in oil; transfer from skillet to a baking dish. Combine remaining ingredients in same skillet and bring to a boil; remove from heat and pour over steak. Bake 1¼ hours, then remove from oven; cool before serving.

Restaurant Recipe

Southwest Chicken

1 chicken breast, trimmed of fat
1 teaspoon Southwest seasoning, divided
½ green bell pepper
½ red bell pepper
¼ onion
1 tablespoon butter
½ cup cooked rice
¼ cup shredded Monterey Jack cheese

Rub chicken breast with ½ teaspoon Southwest seasoning on each side; grill over direct heat until cooked through and internal temperature reads between 165° and 170°. Slice bell peppers and onion into thin ribbons; sauté in butter until crisp but tender. Plate rice with chicken on top, then top with cheese. Spoon peppers and onion over top of chicken. Enjoy!

Restaurant Recipe

White Dog Hill Restaurant

22901 North Route 66
Clinton, OK 73601
580-323-6922
Find us on Facebook

At White Dog Hill Restaurant, you'll discover spectacular sunsets, tasty food, and maybe a supernatural friend. Housed in the former native red-stone clubhouse of the Clinton Country Club, the restaurant sits atop a rising plain above a snaking dirt road. The menu features succulent steaks, juicy fowl, and imaginative salads. Enjoy a meal on the sprawling deck while taking in a gorgeous, unimpeded view that stretches for miles. White Dog Hill Restaurant is also rumored to be home to a ghost named Dottie, who makes her presence known by whispering in diners' ears, moving chairs, and occasionally setting off the security system. Come see for yourself!

Wednesday – Saturday: 5:30 pm to 8:30 pm

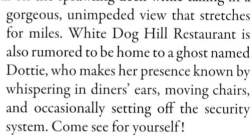

Cinnamon Roll Rum Bread Pudding

6 to 8 cinnamon rolls
6 to 8 pecan swirls
1½ loaves cinnamon bread
½ to ¾ loaf white bread
1 cup raisins
1 cup pecans
7 eggs
⅔ cup brown sugar
⅔ cup white sugar
2½ cups 2% milk
2½ cups buttermilk
¼ cup spiced rum
2 teaspoons vanilla extract
2 teaspoons ground cinnamon
2 teaspoons ground nutmeg
2 ground cloves

Cube rolls, swirls and breads into bite-size pieces. Mix all liquid ingredients and spices in large bowl and stir. Add cubed bread, raisins and pecans. If there is too much liquid, add more cinnamon bread. Let sit 10 to 15 minutes. Pour into a buttered and floured steamer pan. Bake at 350° for 40 to 45 minutes or until bread is puffy and browned on top. Top with glaze.

Glaze:
½ (16-ounce) can vanilla frosting
1 teaspoon ground cinnamon
1 teaspoon sugar
1 teaspoon rum
1 teaspoon maple syrup

Mix all ingredients in a saucepan and warm glaze on stove. Pour over warm bread pudding. Enjoy!

Rosemary Simple Syrup

12 sprigs of rosemary
1 cup water
1 cup turbinado sugar

Steep rosemary in simmering water for at least 7 minutes; add sugar. Gently stir until sugar is dissolved, allow to cool and strain.

Rosemary Collins

1½ ounces London dry gin
½ ounce freshly squeezed lemon juice
½ ounce Rosemary Simple Syrup
(see recipe above)
Club soda
Rosemary sprig for garnish

Shake and strain gin, lemon juice and Rosemary Simple Syrup over fresh ice, top with club soda and garnish with rosemary sprig.

220 Kansas Street
Drummond, OK 73735
580-493-2797
Find us on Facebook

Welcome to Henry's Brake Room, Drummond's hidden gem. Stop by for delicious potato salad, coleslaw, and flaky fried catfish served in a rustic atmosphere. The restaurant also serves fillet, strip, T-bone, ribeyes, and rack of lamb. Enjoy an ice-cold beer with your meal to experience the perfect pairing. Between the accommodating staff and the delicious food, you're sure to have a wonderful time at Henry's Brake Room.

Tuesday, Friday, & Saturday: 5:00 pm to 9:00 pm

Jambalaya

2 whole broiler chickens
1 stick butter
1 tablespoon all-purpose flour
1 cup chopped garlic
3 cups chopped white onion
3 cups chopped green bell pepper
½ cup white wine
3 cups Worcestershire sauce
2 cups soy sauce
3 tablespoons pepper
2 tablespoons salt
1 tablespoon cayenne pepper or to taste
2½ pounds smoked sausage, browned
1 gallon diced tomatoes
Cooked rice for serving
Shredded mozzarella cheese for topping

Add chickens to large stockpot; cover with water and boil 1½ to 2 hours. In a large stockpot over low heat, melt butter; add flour and stir until light brown. Increase heat to medium and add garlic; cook 1 minute until fragrant. Add onion; cook 5 to 7 minutes until translucent. Add bell pepper; cook 5 to 7 minutes until tender. Add wine; once bubbling, add Worcestershire, soy sauce, pepper, salt and cayenne. Remove chickens from stockpot, reserving half of stock; skin, debone and add chicken to roux. Add sausage, tomatoes, and reserved stock; cook over medium-low heat until heated through. Serve over rice; top with mozzarella.

Restaurant Recipe

Smothered Pork Chops

25 potatoes, diced
2 onions, diced
1 pound bacon, chopped
6 tablespoons pepper, divided
4 tablespoons salt, divided
1 tablespoon Lawry's seasoned salt
2 gallons green beans in juice
20 (1¼-inch-thick) pork chops
1 (50-ounce) can cream of
mushroom soup
½ gallon apple juice

In a large stockpot, combine potatoes, onions, bacon, 3 tablespoons pepper, 2 tablespoons salt and Lawry's seasoned salt; strain green bean juice into stockpot and cook over low heat until potatoes are tender. In a separate pot, combine green beans and water to cover; cook over low heat until heated through. In a large roasting pan, combine pork chops, soup, apple juice and remaining pepper and salt; bake at 300° until chops are done. Drain potato mixture and green beans; mix together. Serve chops covered with potato–green bean mixture.

Restaurant Recipe

Tastees Burgers

101 North Highway 81
Duncan, OK 73533
580-252-2558
Find us on Facebook

There's nothing quite like biting into the perfect, juicy burger. At Tastees Burgers, you get the perfect burger experience every time you visit. Serving hamburgers and cheeseburgers six days a week, Tastees is a Duncan staple that provides customers with a tasty meal on demand. The restaurant also offers a variety of sandwiches, salads, hot dogs, and baskets. As for sides, you can't go wrong with freshly cut fries, onion rings, fried pickles, spicy cheese bites, corn nuggets, or any of Tastees' other delicious sides. With so much to offer, Tastees is sure to please your palate, whatever you might be craving.

Monday – Friday: 10:30 am to 7:00 pm
Saturday: 10:30 am to 4:00 pm

Fast Hash

1 (16-ounce) bag frozen cubed potatoes
1 onion, chopped
¼ cup oil
Salt and pepper to taste
½ teaspoon ground sage
1 (16-ounce) can corned beef

In a large skillet over medium heat, lightly brown potatoes and onions in oil, stirring frequently, until almost tender. Add salt and pepper and sage; mix well. Spread corned beef over potatoes and cover. Set to low heat and steam 5 minutes. Remove cover and stir to mix well. Return heat to medium and cook 2 more minutes.

Local Favorite

Pork Chops & Rice

6 pork chops
6 tablespoons rice
6 slices onion
6 slices tomato
6 slices green bell pepper
1 (15-ounce) can chicken stock

Preheat oven to 350°. Brown pork chops on both sides. Grease a casserole dish well. Place 1 tablespoon rice for each pork chop in bottom of casserole dish. Place chops over each mound. Place 1 slice each of onion, tomato and bell pepper on each chop. Cover with chicken stock and bake 1 hour.

Local Favorite

9201 State Highway 17
Building 2, Suite A
Elgin, OK 73538
580-492-1400
www.tinymaes.com • Find us on Facebook

Tiny Mae's Bar & Grill is a family-owned and -operated restaurant serving the Elgin community and visitors alike. Guests will enjoy a full-service bar as well as a menu featuring a selection of items sure to please even the pickiest eater. Tiny

Mae's serves local beef raised in Comanche County, so customers are guaranteed the best taste every time they visit. Dine on burgers, steaks, salads, and so much more. Don't forget to try one of the daily dinner and lunch specials. Try Tiny Mae's Bar & Grill for fun atmosphere, good food, and outstanding customer service.

Tuesday – Thursday: 11:00 am to 9:00 pm
Friday & Saturday: 11:00 am to 11:00 pm

Homemade Chili

2 pounds ground beef
1 onion, chopped
1 green bell pepper, chopped
1 (12-ounce) can tomato paste
1 teaspoon salt
Pepper to taste
1 tablespoon packed brown sugar
½ teaspoon dried thyme
1 tablespoon ground cumin
2 tablespoons garlic powder
1 teaspoon cayenne pepper
1 teaspoon dried oregano
2 bay leaves
1 tablespoon barbecue sauce
2 tablespoons Worcestershire sauce
2 beef bouillon cubes
1 cup red wine

In a Dutch oven over medium heat, sauté beef, onion and bell pepper, stirring often. When meat is browned, add remaining ingredients, along with 2 cups water; bring to a boil. Reduce to low heat and simmer 3 hours, stirring periodically and adding water as needed.

Local Favorite

Marinated Beef Tenderloin

1 cup ketchup
2 teaspoons mustard
½ teaspoon Worcestershire sauce
2 (1-ounce) packages Italian
salad dressing mix
1 (6-pound) beef tenderloin, trimmed

Combine ketchup, mustard, Worcestershire, dressing mix and 1½ cups water in a bowl; mix well. Pierce beef in several places; combine with marinade in heavy-duty, zip-close plastic bag. Marinate in refrigerator at least 8 hours, turning occasionally. Drain, reserving marinade. Preheat oven to 425°. Place beef in a baking pan with a rack; insert meat thermometer. Bake 30 to 45 minutes or until thermometer reaches 140° for rare, 150° for medium-rare or 160° for medium, basting occasionally with reserved marinade.

Local Favorite

MajorBean
coffee & sandwich co.

201 West Broadway Avenue
Elk City, OK 73644
580-243-9488
www.major-bean-coffee.com
Find us on Facebook

Housed in a restored 1906-dated building, Major Bean Coffee & Sandwich Co. offers wonderful coffee and tasty sandwiches to locals and visitors alike. Enjoy coffee sourced from a small roaster that purchases its beans from around the world while you take in the beautiful tin ceiling tiles and red brick. Major Bean uses organic sauces and syrups for its specialty coffee drinks. Also sample breakfast dishes, paninis, wraps, sandwiches, and salads. The restaurant makes use of organic and non-GMO produce wherever possible, so you'll get the freshest taste every visit. Stop by Major Bean today, where they keep it simple and fresh.

Monday, Tuesday, Thursday, & Friday:
7:00 am to 6:00 pm
Wednesday & Saturday: 7:00 am to 5:00 pm

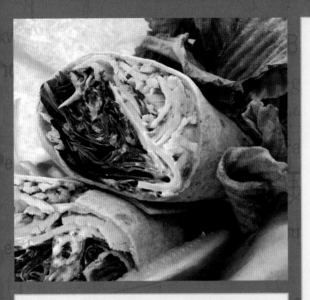

Major's Chicken Salad Wrap

This recipe is measured by taste. Start with these basic ingredients and adjust quantities to your liking.

Cooked chopped chicken breast to taste
Chopped avocado to taste
Chopped fresh cilantro to taste
Chopped red onion to taste
Bacon bits to taste
Mayonnaise to taste
Jalapeño ranch dressing to taste
Spinach tortillas for serving
Baby spinach for serving

In a large bowl, mix chicken, avocado, cilantro, onion, bacon bits, mayonnaise and jalapeño ranch dressing. Adjust ingredient quantities according to your personal taste and with regard to how many people you are serving. Line spinach tortillas with baby spinach; spoon chicken salad into tortillas and wrap. Enjoy.

Restaurant Recipe

Spicy Italian Basil Sandwich

1 ciabatta roll, sliced in half
1 to 2 tablespoons mayonnaise
1 ounce provolone cheese, sliced
2 ounces uncured ham, sliced
1 ounce uncured salami, sliced
1 ounce uncured pepperoni, sliced
¼ red bell pepper, sliced
½ banana pepper, sliced
Chopped fresh basil
1 ounce mozzarella cheese, sliced
1 to 2 tablespoons pesto

On bottom half of ciabatta roll, spread mayonnaise, then layer provolone, ham, salami, pepperoni, bell pepper, banana pepper, basil and mozzarella. On top half of ciabatta roll, spread pesto and top sandwich. Press sandwich on a panini grill or cook in a toaster oven until cheese is melted and bread is crispy. Enjoy.

Restaurant Recipe

PRAIRIEFIRE

PrairieFire Grille

422 South Main Street
Elk City, OK 73644
580-225-6865
www.prairiefireelkcity.com
Find us on Facebook

PrairieFire Grille was opened in October 2011 by Mary Kilhoffer and Amy Vickers, a mother-daughter team who have created a western Oklahoma staple serving good food by good people. Located in the historic MKT train station, PrairieFire Grille has created a unique dining experience by pairing simple ingredients, like fresh vegetables and high-quality meats, with culinary knowledge and skill. The restaurant also boasts a full bar stocked with Oklahoma brews, specialty cocktails, and the classics. The wonderful atmosphere, quality food, and excellent customer service will ensure you enjoy a dining experience to remember.

Lunch:
Monday – Friday: 11:00 am to 2:00 pm
Dinner:
Monday – Saturday: 5:00 pm to 9:00 pm

Dr Pepper Sauce

4½ cups ketchup
6 (12-ounce) cans Dr Pepper
6 tablespoons tomato paste
6 tablespoons Worcestershire sauce
3 teaspoons onion powder
Salt and pepper
1 cup cold water
2 tablespoons cornstarch
Fresh mashed potatoes
Cooked meatballs

In a saucepan over medium-high heat, combine ketchup, Dr Pepper, tomato paste, Worcestershire, onion powder and salt and pepper; bring to a boil, then reduce to a simmer for 15 minutes. In a bowl, combine water and cornstarch; add to sauce to thicken. Plate mashed potatoes and top with meatballs. Ladle sauce over top and serve.

Restaurant Recipe

Prairie Meatballs

4 pounds ground beef
4 pounds hot sausage
4 eggs
4 tablespoons dried parsley
3 cups panko
½ teaspoon kosher salt
1 teaspoon coarse pepper
4 teaspoons olive oil
2 yellow onions, chopped
2 green bell peppers, chopped
4 tablespoons minced garlic

Preheat oven to 350°. In a large bowl, combine meats, eggs, parsley, panko, kosher salt, pepper and olive oil. Add onions, bell peppers and garlic to a food processor and blend until smooth; add to meat mixture and mix well. Roll into 1½-inch meatballs and arrange 2 inches apart on baking sheets. Bake 20 to 30 minutes. Makes about 96 meatballs.

Restaurant Recipe

Farmhouse Fresh

717 South Hoover Street
Enid, OK 73703
580-231-7473
Find us on Facebook

Farmhouse Fresh is a coffee shop and deli serving Enid since January 2018. Community demand for farm-fresh food grew, and Farmhouse Fresh rose to the challenge, eager to fill that void. Using certified, naturally raised meats, eggs, and honey, the restaurant crafts delicious farm-to-fork fare. Enjoy organic teas and coffees, fresh kombuchas, soups, salads, quiche, and sandwiches. Those with dietary requirements will be pleased to learn Farmhouse Fresh accommodates customers who eat vegan, vegetarian, paleo, keto, and gluten-free diets. After your meal, browse the dessert counter for something sweet. With a rotating menu of specials, you'll always find something exciting at Farmhouse Fresh.

Monday – Friday: 7:00 am to 4:00 pm
Saturday: 7:00 am to 2:00 pm

Butternut Squash Chili

½ sweet onion, chopped

3 cloves garlic, chopped

1 tablespoon tallow (or coconut oil)

1 tablespoon chili powder

1 teaspoon ground cumin

1 teaspoon ground ginger

¼ teaspoon ground coriander

¼ teaspoon ground allspice

1 pound grass-fed ground meat of choice

2 stalks celery, chopped

1 green bell pepper, deseeded and diced

6 tomatoes, chopped, seeds and juices reserved

1 butternut squash, peeled, deseeded and chopped

1 teaspoon chopped green chiles

1 cup homemade bone broth of choice

1 tablespoon raw local honey

Chopped green onion, shredded Cheddar cheese and sour cream for garnish

In a large pot over medium heat, sauté onion and garlic in tallow until translucent; add spices and stir 1 minute or until fragrant. Transfer to a plate and brown meat in pot; return onion mixture to pot, add remaining ingredients, cover pot and bring to a boil. Reduce heat to simmer and cook 1 hour, stirring occasionally, until squash is tender. Enjoy with garnishes of green onion, cheese and sour cream.

Restaurant Recipe

Chickpea Salad

2 (15-ounce) cans chickpeas, drained and rinsed

1 avocado, pitted and diced

1 cup halved cherry tomatoes

¼ cup chopped Brussels sprouts

1 cucumber, diced

1 red onion, finely diced

½ cup crumbled feta cheese

¼ cup sliced chives

In a large bowl, combine all ingredients; toss together until evenly distributed.

Dressing:

1 to 2 tablespoons mustard

2 tablespoons red wine vinegar

1 lemon, juiced

1 pinch garlic powder

1 pinch onion powder

1 teaspoon dried parsley

Salt and pepper to taste

¼ cup olive oil

In a food processor, process all ingredients until smooth. Pour over salad and toss gently to coat. Enjoy.

Restaurant Recipe

Urban Bru

418 Northwest 21st Street
Guymon, OK 73942
580-338-3010
www.urbanbru.cafe • Find us on Facebook

Urban Bru is a café committed to serving the best coffee and delicious food. The café has been awarded Certified Healthy Restaurant in the Excellence Category for many years now. Urban Bru's coffee was also voted best in Oklahoma in 2015. Try the Purple Rain latte, a fusion of lavender, coconut, and vanilla. In addition to coffee, the café serves a unique selection of appetizers, soups, and entrées to satisfy every taste, sometimes even offering seasonal dishes. Have your next meal at Urban Bru, where quality is everything.

Monday – Friday: 6:30 am to 5:30 pm
Saturday: 8:00 am to 5:30 pm
Sunday: 8:00 am to 2:00 pm

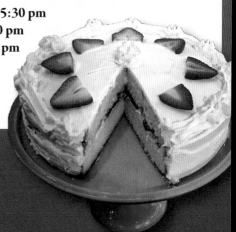

Baked Fish

1 teaspoon dried minced onion
½ teaspoon dry mustard
¼ teaspoon crushed tarragon leaves
Pinch pepper
1½ pounds flounder fillets
Salt to taste
1 teaspoon lemon juice
½ cup mayonnaise
Paprika for garnish

Preheat oven to 425°. Combine onion, mustard, tarragon and pepper with 2 teaspoons warm water; set aside for 10 minutes so flavors can blend. Dry fish and arrange in greased 9x11-inch glass baking dish; sprinkle with salt. Whisk lemon juice and mayonnaise into tarragon mixture; spread over fish. Bake 25 to 30 minutes or until fish is browned and flakes easily. Garnish with paprika.

Local Favorite

Cheddar & Sour Cream Cornbread

½ cup margarine
1½ cups cornmeal
⅓ cup all-purpose flour
4 teaspoons baking powder
½ teaspoon salt
2 eggs, beaten
1 cup sour cream
1 (15-ounce) can cream-style corn
¼ cup grated onion
½ cup shredded Cheddar cheese

Preheat oven to 375°. Heat margarine in a 9x13-inch baking dish until melted. Combine cornmeal, flour, baking powder and salt in a bowl; mix well. Stir in eggs, sour cream, corn, onion and melted margarine; add to baking dish. Bake 40 minutes or until golden brown. Sprinkle cheese over top and return to oven until cheese is melted.

Local Favorite

The Sugar Shak

105 East Cherokee Street
Medford, OK 73759
580-395-3188
Find us on Facebook

The Sugar Shak is a hole-in-the-wall restaurant serving up house-made sandwiches, wraps, pizza, wings, and sno-cones. At the Sugar Shak, all sandwiches are made to order, from turkey

and Swiss to BLTs. Customize your sandwich with your choice of white, wheat, or marble rye bread. You can even order a specialty like the Big Daddy, which features pulled pork, ham, and pepper Jack sandwich on a toasted hoagie bun. The restaurant also makes wraps, each prepared on a jalapeño wrap with the restaurant's tasty Shak Spread. The Sugar Shak proudly serves Hunt Brothers pizza, wings, and WingBites as well, so you can always try something new.

Monday – Saturday: 11:00 am to 8:00 pm
Sunday: 3:00 pm to 8:00 pm

Chicken-Bacon-Ranch Nachos

1 chicken breast fillet, grilled
¼ cup ranch dressing
¼ cup chopped, cooked bacon
Tortilla chips for serving
¼ cup melted queso blanco
¼ cup shredded Cheddar-Jack cheese
Salsa, sour cream and jalapeños for serving

Dice chicken breast, then toss with ranch and bacon in a bowl; marinate 4 to 6 hours. When done, add tortilla chips to a shallow bowl. Top with chicken-bacon-ranch mixture, queso blanco and cheese. Serve with salsa, sour cream and jalapeños.

Restaurant Recipe

Chicken Fajita Wrap

1 chicken breast fillet, grilled
½ green bell pepper, diced
½ onion, diced
1 to 2 tablespoons spicy ranch dressing plus more for serving
1 jalapeño tortilla
2 tablespoons salsa
¼ cup shredded Cheddar-Jack cheese

In a skillet over medium heat, sauté chicken, bell pepper and onion until onion is translucent. Spread spicy ranch over tortilla, then add chicken, bell pepper and onion. Top with salsa and cheese; roll up and toast in the oven until cheese is melted. Serve with spicy ranch for dipping.

Restaurant Recipe

The Old Plantation Restaurant

143 East Lake Drive
Medicine Park, OK 73557
580-529-6262
www.theoldplantationrestaurant.com • Find us on Facebook

Housed in a three-story building built in 1910, The Old Plantation Restaurant opened to the public in 1966. Before it was a restaurant, the building was a hotel that enjoyed raging success in the Roaring Twenties, hosting the likes of Al Capone, Machine Gun Kelly, and

Bonnie and Clyde. During WWII, the hotel closed after falling on hard times. In 1966, Rex and Ruby reopened the hotel as The Old Plantation Restaurant, operating it for thirty-five years before closing in the early 2000s. Today, the restaurant operates under the direction of owners Chad and Jenna Thornton, who serve up traditional southern-style food, great service, and a taste of priceless history.

Daily: 11:00 am to 9:00 pm

Blue Holy Water

½ ounce coconut rum
½ ounce vodka
½ ounce peach schnapps
½ ounce blue curaçao
1 ounce pineapple juice
5 ounces Sprite
1 orange wedge for garnish
1 cherry for garnish

In a shaker, combine rum, vodka, schnapps, curaçao, pineapple juice and Sprite; shake, then strain into an ice-filled 16-ounce mason jar. Garnish with orange wedge and cherry.

Restaurant Recipe

Grandma's Homemade Hot Rolls

1 egg
2¼ teaspoons dry yeast
1 teaspoon salt
½ cup sugar
7 cups flour

In a large bowl, mix all ingredients plus 2 cups lukewarm water; cover and let rise until doubled in size. Turn dough out onto a clean, floured surface; knead down, place into a greased loaf pan and let rise until doubled in size. Preheat oven to 400°. Pinch off sections of dough, rolling into balls of desired size; place on greased baking sheet. Bake 15 to 20 minutes or until golden brown.

Restaurant Recipe

SCREAMIN JACK'S

BBQ and MORE

Located a stone's throw off Route 66
602 Arkansas Avenue
Sayre, OK 73662
580-210-0076
www.screaminjack.com
Find us on Facebook

Welcome to Screamin' Jack's BBQ and More. At Screamin' Jack's, you'll enjoy tried-and-true Oklahoma and Texas recipes, each crafted with ingredients of only the finest quality. The quaint food stand also makes its own spice blends and rubs and handcrafts its sauces in small batches to ensure the signature Screamin' Jack's taste always comes first. Take your pick of various barbecue dinners, tasty sandwiches, jalapeño poppers, green chili, burritos, quesadillas, house-made nachos, street tacos, fries, onion rings, and a selection of delicious sides. If you're feeding a crowd, you can even buy your barbecue by the pound or have your event catered. At Screamin' Jack's BBQ and More, your meal is made to order, every time.

Tuesday – Thursday: 11:00 am to 2:00 pm
Friday: 11:00 am to 6:00 pm

JACK'S
REDNECK TACOS

SMOKED CATFISH DIP

STUFFED CHICKEN POPPER

Jack's Stuffed Chicken Popper

4 jalapeños, halved lengthwise and deseeded

Softened cream cheese as needed

Screamin' Jack's Ultimate Chicken Rub to taste

8 boneless, skinless chicken thighs

8 strips thick bacon

1 stick butter, melted

Screamin' Jack's Original BBQ Sauce to taste

Preheat smoker to 250°. Fill jalapeño halves with cream cheese; sprinkle each with chicken rub. Place jalapeños on top of chicken thighs with cheese sides up. Tightly roll thighs around jalapeño halves and wrap each with 1 strip bacon. Place in smoker for 1 hour. When internal temperature reaches 160°, increase smoker temperature to 300°. Smoke 20 more minutes or until bacon is crisp. Mix butter with BBQ sauce and baste poppers. Enjoy.

Restaurant Recipe

Smoked Catfish Dip

1 jalapeño, deseeded and chopped

1 tablespoon Jack's Sweet Heat rub

1 (8-ounce) package cream cheese, softened

2 teaspoons lemon juice

1 teaspoon garlic powder

1 teaspoon ground celery seed

2 tablespoons chopped sweet onion

1 teaspoon prepared horseradish

4 tablespoons sour cream

2 tablespoons mayonnaise

4 drops Jack's Hot Pepper sauce

3 drops Worcestershire sauce

1 cup smoked, flaked catfish

Chopped fresh dill for garnish

Crackers or chips for serving

Mix together all ingredients except catfish, dill and crackers in a large bowl. Fold in catfish until combined. Cover and refrigerate 2 hours. Garnish with dill and serve with your favorite crackers or chips.

Restaurant Recipe

Bait Shop Burgers

701 E Street
Snyder, OK 73566
580-569-2021
Find us on Facebook

At Bait Shop Burgers, the ultimate mission is always to ensure that customers get the best food possible. Unlike chain restaurants, Bait Shop Burgers prepares its delicious fare using

real, fresh ingredients. Each burger is made with a 100 percent real beef patty and assembled with fresh vegetables, so you don't have to worry about putting chemicals from fake products into your body. The burger joint also offers breakfast and a variety of catfish dinners, shrimp dinners, burritos, and tacos. Stop by Bait Shop Burgers for quality food and unmatched service.

Monday & Wednesday – Sunday: 7:00 am to 8:00 pm

Baked Potato Soup

⅔ cup butter
⅔ cup self-rising flour
6 cups milk
4 potatoes, baked and halved
Chopped onion to taste, optional
8 slices bacon, cooked and
crumbled, divided
1 cup sour cream
Grated Cheddar cheese for topping

In a large saucepan, melt butter; add flour and stir until smooth. Whisk in milk and cook until heated through. Scoop out pulp from potatoes; discard skins and add pulp to saucepan along with onion and half of bacon. Stir in sour cream. When hot, sprinkle with cheese and remaining bacon.

Restaurant Recipe

Bunch of Banana Bread

1½ cups all-purpose flour
1¼ teaspoons baking powder
½ teaspoon baking soda
½ teaspoon ground cinnamon
⅛ teaspoon salt
2 egg whites, slightly beaten
1 cup (about 3) mashed ripe bananas
¾ cup sugar
¼ cup vegetable oil

Preheat oven to 350°. In a medium bowl, whisk together flour, baking powder, baking soda, cinnamon and salt; set aside. In a large bowl, stir together egg whites, bananas, sugar and oil. Add dry ingredients to banana mixture and stir until just moistened. Batter will be lumpy. Pour into a greased 4½x8½-inch loaf pan; bake 30 to 45 minutes or until toothpick inserted into center comes out clean. Cool before removing from pan.

Restaurant Recipe

Doug's Peach Orchard

27677 US Highway 81
Terral, OK 73569
580-437-2366
Find us on Facebook

Doug's Peach Orchard has served the Terral area for more than seventy years. First opened in 1948, the restaurant offers some of the tastiest country-style fare in Oklahoma. Diners will enjoy mouthwatering menu items like catfish, steak fingers, freshly cut fries, chicken livers, hushpuppies, fried pickles, shrimp, and so much more. Doug's Peach Orchard is known for its world-famous tartar sauce, the recipe for which is top secret. You'll have to visit if you want a taste. After your meal, a slice of delicious homemade pie is the perfect way to cap your experience. Get lost in the rustic, small-town atmosphere while you enjoy a no-frills meal with an ice-cold beer.

Tuesday – Sunday: 11:00 am to 8:45 pm

Cherry Mash

1 stick margarine
2 cups sugar
1 pinch salt
¾ cup evaporated milk
18 large marshmallows
1 (10-ounce) bag cherry chips
12 ounces milk chocolate chips
¾ cup creamy peanut butter
1 pound roasted peanuts, chopped
1 teaspoon vanilla extract

In a saucepan, combine margarine, sugar, salt and milk; bring to a boil. Cook 5 minutes, stirring to prevent scorching. Remove from heat; stir in marshmallows and cherry chips until smooth. Cool slightly and press cherry mixture into a buttered heat-safe dish. In a microwave-safe bowl, combine chocolate chips and peanut butter; microwave in intervals, stirring every 30 seconds until smooth. Stir in peanuts and vanilla, then pour over top of cherry layer. Refrigerate 2 hours until set, then cut into squares.

Family Favorite

Chocolate Fudge

1 stick margarine
12 large marshmallows
2 cups sugar
1 dash salt
½ cup evaporated milk
6 ounces semisweet chocolate chips
1 cup chopped pecans
1 teaspoon vanilla extract

In a saucepan, combine margarine, marshmallows, sugar, salt and milk; bring to a boil. Cook, stirring frequently, until marshmallows are melted. Stir in chocolate chips until melted. Stir in pecans and vanilla. Pour mixture into a buttered heat-safe dish; set aside in a cool place until completely cooled. Cut into squares and enjoy.

Family Favorite

Marshall's Joint

112 East Broadway Street
Vici, OK 73859
580-747-6899
Find us on Facebook

Serving Vici since 2010, Marshall's Joint offers some of the best smoked meats around. From ribs to chicken to sausage, Marshall's Joint smokes it all. Guests will also enjoy tasty sides like jambalaya, red-skinned tater salad, green chile hominy, and slaw. For diners on the go, Marshall's Joint also offers a variety of wraps, burritos, and quesadillas. Satisfy your sweet tooth with your choice of cobbler, brownies, ice cream, or soda floats. There is also a junior menu, so don't forget to bring the kiddos when you visit. Visit Marshall's Joint, where they're always smokin' the good stuff.

Monday – Thursday: 11:00 am to 7:00 pm
Friday: 11:00 am to 2:30 pm

Marshall's Basic Meat Prep

This method of meat preparation will work with your meat of choice every time. Try pork butt, round roast, chicken breast, chicken thigh, sausage, hot links, beef brisket and more.

Garlic powder
Freshly ground pepper
Salt
Other choice seasonings, optional
Your meat of choice

In a bowl, toss together 2 parts garlic powder to 2 parts pepper to 1 part salt. This 2:2:1 ratio is Marshall's basic rub. Depending on the cut or your taste, you may add additional seasonings to taste. Coat meat with rub, massaging it in to ensure flavor. Smoke between 225° and 240° in smoker over oak wood or slow roast in oven between 200° and 250° until meat reaches desired tenderness or internal temperature required for doneness. Enjoy.

Restaurant Recipe

Jambalaya

8 cups raw long-grain whole-grain rice
4 to 5 onions, chopped
½ to 1 stalk celery, chopped
1 to 2 green bell peppers, chopped
1 head garlic, cloves separated and minced
¼ cup cooking oil
1 (102-ounce) can diced tomatoes
1 (106-ounce) can tomato sauce
10 or 12 dashes Creole seasoning
10 or 12 dashes six-pepper salt
10 dashes pepper
2 dashes cayenne pepper
Cooked meat of choice (chicken, smoked sausage, etc.), optional

In a large stockpot, bring 8 cups water to a boil. Add rice, reduce to a simmer and cover, cooking 45 minutes or until tender; add water as needed. In a large stockpot over medium-high heat, sauté onions, celery, bell peppers and garlic in oil until softened. Add remaining ingredients to sautéed veggies, reduce to a simmer and cook 30 minutes. Add cooked rice to mixture and stir until well combined.

Restaurant Recipe

Dubtown Grill

4200 Carriage Way
Weatherford, OK 73096
580-774-2216
www.okhealthandwellness.com/dubtowngrill
Find us on Facebook

Dubtown Grill is the hidden gem of restaurants in Weatherford. Located inside the Oklahoma Health and Wellness Center, just off of Exit 84 at I-40 and Airport Road, Dubtown Grill offers a selection of southern classics that delight locals and travelers alike. The menu includes specialty burgers, wraps, salads, and dinner entrées with delicious sides. The restaurant also provides vegan options, such as the Beyond Burger, and all menu items are customizable to your individual diet specifications.

Monday – Saturday: 10:00 am to 8:00 pm

Broccoli Salad

5 cups chopped broccoli florets
1 cup shelled sunflower seeds
1 cup Hormel bacon pieces
¼ cup chopped red onion
1 cup raisins

In a medium bowl, toss together all ingredients until well combined.

Dressing:

1 cup mayonnaise
2 tablespoons vinegar
½ cup sugar

In a bowl, combine all ingredients, mixing until smooth. Add Dressing to salad just before serving.

Restaurant Recipe

Homemade Bierocks

1½ pounds ground beef

1 head cabbage, shredded

1 yellow onion, chopped

1 tablespoon pepper

1 tablespoon garlic salt

1 (24-count) package frozen Rhodes Bake-N-Serv® Texas Rolls, thawed

In a large skillet over medium-high heat, brown ground beef and drain. Reduce heat to medium and add cabbage, onion, pepper and garlic salt; cook until cabbage is tender. Stuff each roll with ½ cup to 1 cup cabbage-beef filling and arrange on a baking sheet. Let rise 30 minutes. Meanwhile, preheat oven to 350°. Bake Bierocks 15 to 20 minutes or until browned.

Restaurant Recipe

Mexican Caviar

¼ cup olive oil

1½ tablespoons Tabasco sauce

¼ cup red wine vinegar

¼ teaspoon salt

2 (15.25-ounce) cans whole-kernel corn, drained

2 tomatoes, diced

2 bundles green onions, chopped

2 (15.25-ounce) cans black beans, drained and rinsed

2 avocados, pitted and diced

2 tablespoons chopped fresh cilantro

Tortilla chips for serving

In a small bowl, whisk together oil, Tabasco, vinegar and salt; set aside. In a medium bowl, combine remaining ingredients except tortilla chips; fold until evenly combined and pour oil mixture over top. Refrigerate overnight. Serve with tortilla chips.

Family Favorite

MOTHER OF THE MOTHER ROAD

LUCILLE'S
ROADHOUSE

HISTORIC HIGHWAY 66

1301 North Airport Road
Weatherford, OK 73096
580-772-8808
www.lucillesroadhouse.com • Find us on Facebook

Since 2006, Lucille's Roadhouse has been a part of western Oklahoma's Route 66 tradition. The diner boasts three uniquely decorated seating areas, so regardless of mood or number of party, you can find a spot to enjoy your meal. Wherever you sit, you'll be transported back in time to the glory days of America's Main Street. You'll enjoy famous scratch-made fare like juicy steaks, sandwiches, and other grilled specialties. Come down to Lucille's Roadhouse, enjoy a delicious meal, kick back in the lounge, and enjoy the largest selection of handcrafted Oklahoma beers this side of I-35.

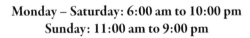

Monday – Saturday: 6:00 am to 10:00 pm
Sunday: 11:00 am to 9:00 pm

Red Rice

14 slices bacon
2 red bell peppers, chopped
1 onion, chopped
4 teaspoons dried thyme
1 cup tomato paste
3 cups uncooked long-grain rice
6 cups chicken stock
1 tablespoon Tabasco sauce

In a large skillet over medium heat, fry bacon until crisp; remove from skillet, drain on paper towels and crumble. Leave 3 tablespoons bacon drippings in skillet over medium heat. Add bell peppers, onion and thyme; sauté 5 minutes. Mix in bacon, tomato paste, rice, stock and Tabasco. Reduce heat, cover and simmer 30 minutes or until rice is tender.

Local Favorite

Ham & Corn Chowder

2 cups diced, cooked ham
1 cup chopped celery
½ cup chopped onion
½ cup butter
3 (10-ounce) packages frozen
cream-style corn, thawed
1 cup milk
½ teaspoon onion salt
½ teaspoon celery salt
½ teaspoon pepper
Chopped fresh parsley for garnish

In a Dutch oven over medium heat, sauté ham, celery and onion in butter. Stir in corn, milk, onion salt, celery salt and pepper. Bring to a boil, reduce heat to low and simmer, stirring occasionally, 20 minutes. Plate and garnish with parsley.

Local Favorite

Café Paradee

A COFFEE CULTURE

Café Paradee

1018 Main Street
Woodward, OK 73801
580-256-8400
www.cafeparadee.com • Find us on Facebook

Café Paradee is a coffee shop that concentrates on providing customers with Haitian coffee and a safe, friendly, inviting place to meet friends or to read a book. The café's coffee is direct,

sustainable trade. It is Café Paradee's goal to have a relationship with the Haitian farmers who provide the coffee. With each cup they serve, the café keeps in mind that there are real faces and stories behind the scenes, enabling the café's customers to enjoy their morning liquid gold. For that, Café Paradee is grateful. Coffee brings people together. Coffee brings out the love. Café Paradee is a coffee culture.

Monday – Friday: 8:30 am to 3:30 pm

Lavender- & Honey-Infused Shortbreads

2 teaspoons dried lavender
1 tablespoon honey
2 sticks unsalted butter
1½ cups powdered sugar
1 teaspoon vanilla extract
¼ teaspoon pink Himalayan salt
2 cups unbleached flour
⅛ cup coarse raw sugar for sprinkling

Break up lavender with fingers and add to a bowl with honey and 1 teaspoon water; microwave 15 seconds and set aside. In a bowl, cream together butter, powdered sugar, vanilla and salt with a handheld electric mixer until light and fluffy; stir in lavender mixture. Stir in flour. Scoop out walnut-size balls of dough and arrange on a baking sheet lined with parchment paper; press down with a fork and sprinkle with raw sugar. Refrigerate 30 minutes. Bake at 350° for 10 to 12 minutes, 1 baking sheet at a time. Let cool and enjoy.

Restaurant Recipe

Northeastern

Waterway Café at

SAFE HARBOR
— HARBORS VIEW —

451107 East 320 Road
Afton, OK 74331
918-782-0445
www.harborsviewmarina.com • Find us on Facebook

Located at Safe Harbor, Harbors View Marina, Waterway Café is a nostalgic reminder of the past. Overlooking the beautiful waters of Grand Lake, the café offers breakfast and lunch on the water with your choice of dining indoors or alfresco on the docks. All meals are made fresh to order and prepared before your eyes by an experienced cook. Waterway Café also includes an old-fashioned soda fountain featuring refreshing treats, like hand-dipped ice cream cones, shakes, malts, sundaes, and Hawaiian shaved ice. Visit Waterway Café for Friday night all-you-can-eat Cajun shrimp boils and Saturday all-you-can-eat fajitas from Memorial Day to Labor Day.

Saturday & Sunday: 9:00 am to 4:00 pm

Cheesy Kielbasa Potatoes

2 links kielbasa sausage, diced

¼ to ½ cup diced onion

¼ cup diced green chiles

**2 pounds red potatoes,
quartered and boiled**

**2 cups shredded Cheddar cheese plus
more for topping**

1 teaspoon pepper supreme

1 teaspoon garlic salt

Preheat oven to 350°. In a greased 9x13-inch baking dish, combine sausage, onion, chiles, potatoes and cheese and sprinkle with pepper supreme and garlic salt. Top with additional cheese, cover with foil and bake until cheese is melted. Remove from oven and set aside for a few minutes before serving.

Restaurant Recipe

Ginger Pancakes with Lemon–Butter Sauce

2 cups pancake mix

1½ cups milk plus more as needed

1 egg, beaten

4 tablespoons molasses

1½ teaspoons ground ginger

½ teaspoon ground cloves

In a bowl, whisk together all ingredients until combined. Drop batter onto a greased hot griddle or skillet with a ¼-cup measuring cup; flip once when bubbles appear on surface. Cook until both sides are golden brown.

Lemon–Butter Sauce:

1 stick butter

4 tablespoons hot water

1 teaspoon lemon zest

1 egg, beaten

1 cup sugar

⅛ cup lemon juice or to taste

In a skillet over low heat, melt butter with water and lemon zest. Add egg, sugar and lemon juice, whisking until combined. Serve over Ginger Pancakes.

Family Favorite

Painted Horse
BAR & GRILLE™

110 Southwest Frank Phillips Boulevard
Bartlesville, OK 74003
918-336-1100
www.painted-horse.com • Find us on Facebook

Welcome to Painted Horse Bar & Grille, a traditional steakhouse with a modern twist. At Painted Horse, it's believed that there are three essentials to operating a restaurant: a cool, old historic building, quality food and beverages, and great service staff. And Painted Horse has it all! The restaurant has also partnered with Wolf Creek Ranch to bring customers locally raised, guaranteed Angus beef products. From ranch to table,

customers will receive the best beef available every time. Don't forget to have a drink at the bar, which boasts a variety of options, from draft beer to featured wines. The staff at Painted Horse Bar & Grille await your visit.

Coffee Bar:
Monday – Friday: 9:00 am to 9:00 pm
Saturday: 10:30 am to 9:00 pm
Kitchen:
Monday – Saturday: 10:30 am to 9:00 pm
Bar:
Monday – Thursday: 10:30 am to 10:00 pm
Friday & Saturday: 10:30 am to midnight

Moscow Mule

**1½ ounces Indian Grass
Oklahoma vodka**

1 lime, juiced

Bundaberg ginger beer

In a copper mug, stir together vodka and lime juice. Top off with ginger beer; stir until combined. Enjoy.

Restaurant Recipe

BBQ Sauce

2 cups ketchup

1 cup honey

1 cup molasses

¼ cup liquid smoke

**¼ cup ghost pepper sauce or your favorite
hot sauce**

1½ teaspoons pepper

1½ teaspoons garlic powder

¼ cup mustard

1 tablespoon sugar

Fill the bottom of a double boiler with water and bring to a boil. Reduce to medium heat, add all ingredients to top pot and cook 1 hour, stirring occasionally.

Restaurant Recipe

Cheri Ann's Trattoria

423 North Main Street
Broken Arrow, OK 74012
918-251-0221
Find us on Facebook

Located in the Rose District of downtown Broken Arrow, Cheri Ann's Trattoria is a family-owned Italian restaurant focused on providing delicious food made with fresh, seasonal

ingredients. The restaurant serves classic entrées like certified Angus New York strip, spaghetti with house marinara, chicken parmigiana, pork loin chops, and more. Guests can also enjoy the soup of the day and a choice of Italian Cobb salad or Greek salad. After the perfect meal, cap your visit with a slice of cheesecake made from a fourth-generation family recipe. Visit Cheri Ann's Trattoria to discover the wholesome taste of scratch-made Italian fare.

Tuesday – Saturday: 4:00 pm to 9:00 pm
Sunday: 11:00 am to 4:00 pm

Bruschetta

2 pounds fresh Roma tomatoes

4 cloves garlic, divided

3 tablespoons extra virgin olive oil plus
more for brushing

¼ cup chopped fresh parsley

Sea salt and pepper to taste

1 baguette

Freshly grated Parmesan
cheese for topping

Dice tomatoes into ¼-inch pieces, then mince 2 cloves garlic. In a bowl, combine tomatoes, garlic, olive oil, parsley and salt and pepper; mix well and let stand 1 hour at room temperature. Preheat oven to 375°. Slice baguette into ½-inch-thick slices; brush with olive oil and arrange on a baking sheet. Bake 7 to 9 minutes or until toasted; remove from oven and rub each slice with remaining garlic cloves. When slices have cooled, top with tomato mixture and garnish with Parmesan. Enjoy.

Restaurant Recipe

Chicken Piccata

2 boneless, skinless chicken breasts

Sea salt and pepper to taste

All-purpose flour for dredging

4 tablespoons unsalted butter, divided

4 tablespoons extra virgin olive oil

2 lemons, juiced

¼ cup chicken stock

¼ cup white wine

2 tablespoons brined capers, rinsed

2 tablespoons chopped fresh parsley

Butterfly chicken breasts but cut all the way through, separating halves completely. Season each with salt and pepper on both sides, then dredge in flour; shake off excess flour and set aside. In a large skillet over medium-high heat, melt 2 tablespoons butter with olive oil. Add chicken to skillet and cook 3 to 4 minutes or until browned; flip and cook 3 minutes more until other sides are browned. Transfer chicken to a plate. To same skillet, add lemon juice, stock, wine and capers; bring to a boil 1 minute, scraping browned bits from bottom. Reduce heat to medium, add chicken back to skillet and simmer 3 to 5 minutes. Transfer chicken to a serving platter, then add remaining butter to skillet, stirring until melted. Pour sauce over chicken and garnish with parsley.

Restaurant Recipe

Shiloh's Restaurant

2604 North Aspen Avenue
Broken Arrow, OK 74012
918-254-1500
www.shilohsrestaurant.com
Find us on Facebook

Shiloh's Restaurant is a family restaurant committed to providing a family-friendly atmosphere, fast and friendly service, and some of the best food in town. When it comes to feeding your family, nothing beats a home-cooked meal, and Shiloh's family recipes bring the taste of home to the dinner table. The restaurant makes everything the way Grandma used to make it. The scratch-made rolls, pies, and cakes are always a hit. Look no further for the best chicken-fried steak, hand-battered chicken tenders, and fried catfish in town. Shiloh's has something for everyone in the family. Drop by and sample their family-favorite dishes today.

Monday – Saturday: 7:00 am to 9:00 pm
Sunday: 7:00 am to 3:00 pm

Strawberry–Rhubarb Pie

2 cups chopped frozen rhubarb
2 cups sliced fresh strawberries
2 cups sugar plus more for dusting
6 tablespoons cornstarch
2 (9-inch) deep-dish pie crusts
2 tablespoons melted butter

Preheat oven to 350°. In a saucepan over low heat, combine rhubarb, strawberries, sugar and cornstarch; cook, stirring occasionally, until thickened. Pour filling into first pie crust; carefully place second crust over pie, pressing edges to seal. Brush top of pie with butter, then dust with sugar. Place pie on a lined baking sheet; bake 45 to 50 minutes or until golden brown.

Restaurant Recipe

Buttermilk Brownies

½ cup butter
½ cup vegetable oil
2 cups all-purpose flour
2½ cups sugar
¼ cup cocoa powder
1 teaspoon baking soda
½ cup buttermilk
2 eggs, beaten

Preheat oven to 400°. In a saucepan, combine butter and vegetable oil with 1 cup water; bring to a boil. In a mixing bowl, combine flour, sugar and cocoa powder; carefully add butter mixture, stirring well. In a bowl, whisk baking soda into buttermilk until dissolved; add to batter, stirring well. Cool batter, then stir in eggs until combined. Pour batter into a 9x13-inch baking dish; bake 15 minutes or until edges are set. Cool before slicing.

Restaurant Recipe

2000 West Reno Street
Broken Arrow, OK 74012
918-258-4227
www.stonemillbbq.com • Find us on Facebook

Steve and Debbie love barbecue. In fact, they once had three homemade smokers in their backyard they'd fire up for family cookouts. In 2003, they transformed their passion into something the whole community could enjoy, building Stone Mill BBQ and Steakhouse

from the ground up. At Stone Mill, you'll find hand-cut steaks, homemade sides and desserts, and tasty slow-smoked barbecue. The restaurant is also particular about quality, so you can always trust they're serving you the absolute best. Bring your family and friends and settle down to a delicious plate of barbecue.

Monday – Thursday: 11:00 am to 8:30 pm
Friday & Saturday: 11:00 am to 9:30 pm
Sunday: 11:00 am to 2:30 pm

Stone Mill Coleslaw

20 pounds cabbage, chopped
4 cups diced carrot
8 cups mayonnaise
4 cups sugar
4 cups milk
8 cups honey mustard
4 tablespoons pepper

In a large bowl, combine cabbage and carrot; set aside. In another bowl, combine remaining ingredients; whisk together until well combined. Add dressing mixture to cabbage and carrots and toss until evenly coated. Refrigerate before serving.

Restaurant Recipe

Chicken Tortilla Soup

3 tablespoons olive oil
1½ cups diced red onion
1½ cups diced celery
1½ cups dicedcarrot
8 tomatoes, oven-roasted with olive oil, peeled and diced
1½ tablespoons diced jalapeño
4 tablespoons minced garlic
4 pounds cooked chicken breasts, diced
1½ bunches fresh cilantro, chopped
¾ cup chicken base
3 tablespoons Cajun seasoning
3 limes, juiced
2 cups cooked whole-kernel corn
2 cups cooked black beans

In a large stockpot, heat olive oil; sauté onion, celery, carrot and tomatoes 5 to 7 minutes. Add jalapeño, garlic, chicken and cilantro; sauté 12 minutes. Add chicken base, Cajun seasoning and 1½ gallons water; simmer 30 minutes. Add lime juice, corn and beans; cook until heated through. Enjoy.

Restaurant Recipe

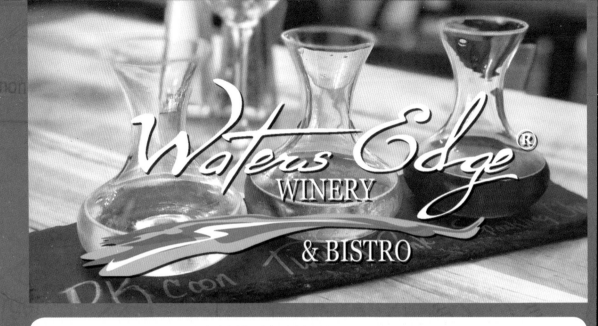

Waters Edge Winery & Bistro

116 South Main Street
Broken Arrow, OK 74011
918-286-0086
www.wewba.com • Find us on Facebook

Waters Edge Winery & Bistro is an urban winery and eatery located in the heart of the Rose District. Owners Michelle and Brian Dean are passionate about wine. Guests will enjoy a variety of wines as well as food inspired by wine country. All wines are made locally using only the finest fruits selected through rigorous inspection. Waters Edge features more than

thirty different wines and varietals, each crafted by an inspired winemaker. The bistro menu is curated to complement every wine offered. Sample meat and cheese boards, paninis, flatbreads, salads, and a selection of wonderful desserts. Live life at the edge with Waters Edge Winery & Bistro.

Tuesday & Wednesday: 11:00 am to 9:00 pm
Thursday – Saturday: 11:00 am to 10:00 pm
Sunday: 11:00 am to 8:00 pm

Pecan Meltaways

1 cup butter, softened
½ cup powdered sugar plus
more for coating
1 teaspoon vanilla extract
2¼ cups all-purpose flour
¼ teaspoon salt
¾ cup chopped pecans

In a large bowl, cream together butter and sugar until light and fluffy; beat in vanilla. In a bowl, combine flour and salt; gradually stir into creamed mixture. Stir in pecans. Refrigerate until chilled. Preheat oven to 350°. Roll dough into 1-inch balls; place on ungreased baking sheets. Bake 10 to 12 minutes or until set. Roll warm cookies in powdered sugar; cool completely on wire racks. Roll cooled cookies again in powdered sugar.

Local Favorite

Oklahoma Salsa

1 (15-ounce) can black-eyed peas
1 (15-ounce) can black beans,
rinsed and drained
1 (15-ounce) can whole-kernel
corn, drained
½ cup chopped onion
½ cup chopped green bell pepper
1 (4-ounce) can diced jalapeños
1 (14.5-ounce) can diced
tomatoes, drained
1 cup Italian salad dressing
½ teaspoon garlic salt

In a medium bowl, combine black-eyed peas, black beans, corn, onion, bell pepper, jalapeño and tomatoes. Season with Italian-style salad dressing and garlic salt; mix well. Cover and refrigerate overnight to blend flavors.

Local Favorite

Hammett House Restaurant

1616 West Will Rogers Boulevard
Claremore, OK 74017
918-341-7333
www.hammetthouse.com • Find us on Facebook

Hammett House Restaurant opened its doors in 1969 after almost twenty years of dreaming and planning on the part of Mrs. LaNelle Hammett. It operated under Mrs. Hammett for many years until 1991, when Bill and Linda Biard purchased the restaurant. Ever since, this Claremore landmark has continued the tradition of providing guests with fine food, exceptional service, restful atmosphere, and, of course, plenty of Oklahoma hospitality. Guests will enjoy homemade soups and hot mashed-potato rolls as well as house-made salad dressings, like the spicy garlic dressing and the cilantro-lime ranch. Don't forget to try one of their famous pies. The team at Hammett House Restaurant can't wait to serve you.

Tuesday – Saturday: 11:00 am to 9:00 pm
Sunday: 11:00 am to 8:00 pm

Lemon-Pecan Pie

6 eggs
½ stick butter, melted
2¼ cups sugar
1 tablespoon lemon juice
1½ teaspoons lemon extract
1 (10-inch) frozen pie crust, thawed
2 cups chopped (or halved) pecans

Preheat oven to 350°. In a large mixing bowl, whisk together eggs, butter, sugar, lemon juice and lemon extract until frothy; pour into pie crust. Top with pecans, taking care to cover the entire surface. Bake 15 minutes, remove from oven and cover with foil. Reduce oven temperature to 300°, then bake pie 30 minutes or until crust is browned and filling is set. Test center of pie for doneness. Let pie sit 30 to 45 minutes at room temperature. Refrigerate until ready to serve.

Restaurant Recipe

German Chocolate Pie

4 cups milk
1½ cups sugar
1 pinch salt
¾ cup cornstarch
5 egg yolks
¾ stick butter
1 teaspoon vanilla extract
½ cup chocolate chips
1⅓ cups shredded coconut, divided
1⅓ cups pecans, divided
1 (10-inch) pie crust, baked
4 cups whipped cream
Chocolate syrup as needed

In a saucepan, heat milk to a scald; whisk in dry ingredients. In a bowl, whisk egg yolks while adding 1 cup hot milk; add to saucepan and boil 1 minute, stirring constantly until thickened. Stir in butter, vanilla, chocolate chips and 1 cup each coconut and pecans. Cool and pour into pie crust. In a bowl, mix whipped cream with chocolate syrup until light brown; fold in remaining coconut and pecans. Spread over pie, making a dome about 6 inches high. Make a lattice design over top with syrup, then refrigerate at least 1 hour.

Restaurant Recipe

Dixie's Cafe

111 North Broadway Street
Coweta, OK 74429
918-279-6830
www.dixiescafeandcatering.com
Find us on Facebook

Dixie's Cafe is a home-style restaurant serving feel-good food as well as catering services to the Coweta community. Created on a foundation of food, family, and faith, the eatery is run by a mother-daughter duo: Dixie Olson and her daughter and business partner, Amanda Mafemi. At Dixie's, you'll enjoy hand-breaded chicken-fried steaks, chicken tenders, and catfish. Only the freshest hand-chopped, hand-sliced vegetables are used in dishes and salads to ensure quality of taste. The eatery also makes its own barbecue sauces, salad dressings, salsas, gravies, soups, chilis, and so much more. Stop in at Dixie's for a home-cooked meal just like your mother used to make.

Tuesday – Friday: 7:00 am to 2:00 pm
Saturday: 7:00 am to 1:00 pm

Sweet French Toast

6 eggs, whisked
2 tablespoons vanilla extract
1 teaspoon ground cinnamon
Butter as needed
12 slices bread of choice
(Texas toast, French bread, etc.)
Powdered sugar for sprinkling
Hot maple syrup for serving
Chopped pecans for topping, optional

Preheat griddle. In a bowl, whisk together eggs, vanilla, cinnamon and 2 tablespoons water. Butter griddle, then place bread 1 slice at a time into egg mixture, turning to coat each side. Place on hot griddle and cook until golden brown; flip and continue cooking other side until golden brown. Plate Sweet French Toast and top with powdered sugar, maple syrup and pecans. Enjoy.

Restaurant Recipe

Egg Salad–BLT Wrap

1 dozen eggs, scrambled
2 stalks celery, diced
¼ white onion, diced
½ cup sweet relish
½ cup Miracle Whip
1 teaspoon mustard
1 teaspoon sugar
1 pinch salt
1 pinch pepper
6 (10-inch) flour tortillas
12 slices bacon, cooked crisp
3 cups shredded lettuce, divided
1½ cups diced tomato, divided

In a large bowl, fold together eggs, celery, onion, relish, Miracle Whip, mustard, sugar, salt and pepper. Divide into 6 even portions and place on tortillas. Place 2 slices bacon on each tortilla, followed by ½ cup lettuce each and ¼ cup tomato each. Roll up each tortilla and serve.

Restaurant Recipe

Garden Gate
Tearoom & Bakery

103 North Main Street
Gore, OK 74435
918-489-2680
Find us on Facebook

Located in downtown Gore, Garden Gate Tearoom & Bakery is the perfect destination for travelers who love a home-cooked meal. The tearoom is known for its flavorful quiche and bread pudding and also offers a full-service espresso bar.

Enjoy sandwiches, soups, and salads featuring house-made dressings as well. Stay for dessert and be sure to try the various dessert cakes. Next to the tearoom is the Garden Gate Shop, a store full of antique and contemporary home furnishings, trinkets, and art. Stop by for a delicious meal and leave with a souvenir from the Garden Gate Shop to commemorate your experience.

Tuesday – Friday: 11:00 am to 2:00 pm
Saturday: 11:00 am to 3:00 pm

Tomato-Basil Soup

1 cup butter
10 slices bacon
6 tomatoes, diced
3 cups chopped yellow onion
1½ cups all-purpose flour
1 gallon chicken stock
1 (106-ounce) can tomato sauce
3 bay leaves
Salt and pepper to taste
¼ cup sugar
Pinch ground nutmeg
3 cups heavy cream

In a large stockpot, melt butter over medium-high heat. Add bacon and cook 3 minutes. Add tomatoes and onion; cook until onion is golden brown. Remove from heat and cool; transfer to a food processor, then blend until smooth. Return to pot and bring to a simmer; add flour and cook 1 minute. Slowly stream in chicken stock and bring to a simmer. Add tomato sauce, bay leaves, salt and pepper, sugar and nutmeg. Return to a simmer and add cream. Simmer 30 minutes.

Restaurant Recipe

Coconut Cream Pie

5 eggs, separated
2 cups evaporated milk
1 cup plus 2 tablespoons sugar, divided
2 tablespoons flour
Dash salt
1 cup shredded coconut, divided
1 teaspoon vanilla extract
1 (9-inch) frozen pie crust, thawed
Pinch cream of tartar

In a large saucepan, combine egg yolks, evaporated milk, 1 cup sugar, flour and salt; stir constantly over high heat until a full boil is reached. Remove from heat and stir in ½ cup coconut and vanilla; pour mixture into pie crust. In a bowl, beat egg whites with cream of tartar using a handheld electric mixer until frothy; add remaining 2 tablespoons sugar and continue beating until stiff peaks form. Spread over top of pie and top with remaining ½ cup coconut. Bake at 350° for 8 minutes or until golden brown.

Restaurant Recipe

SODA STEVE'S

445889 Highway 10A
Gore, OK 74435
918-487-9812
www.sodasteves.com

You'll discover a culinary gem like no other located at Lake Tenkiller. Soda Steve's is a casual, interesting vacation-food eatery created by certified executive chef Steve Pool. The restaurant blends coffee, great music, and a mirror ball situated above a 1920s claw-foot tub in the middle of the dining room. This atmosphere makes Soda Steve's a fun place to grab a bite in the summer heat. You'll enjoy freshly ground burgers, grilled chicken breasts, cheese fries, nachos, creative salads, and old-school sandwiches, like Monte Cristos and fantastic Reubens. Follow up with soft-serve ice cream, hot fudge nachos, shakes, or house-made root beer served in a frosty mug. And yes, their food actually looks like the pictures!

Call ahead for hours
April – October
Monday – Thursday: 11:00 am to 9:00 pm
Friday – Sunday: 11:00 am to 10:00 pm

Soda Steve's 2-Minute Guac

2 pounds fresh avocado pulp
2 tablespoons lime juice
¾ cup diced onion
½ cup diced tomato
1 tablespoon diced jalapeño
2 tablespoons chopped fresh cilantro
1 tablespoon minced garlic
1 tablespoon kosher salt
Pepper to taste

To a bowl, add avocado pulp; add lime juice and toss to prevent avocado turning brown. Using a fork or a potato masher, mash avocado to desired consistency (you may leave some chunks for texture or mash until completely smooth). Add veggies, cilantro and garlic to avocado; fold in until well combined. Season with salt and pepper. Taste and adjust seasonings as needed.

Restaurant Recipe

Poppy Seed Dressing

1½ cups sugar
2 teaspoons dry mustard
2 teaspoons salt
⅔ cup vinegar
3 tablespoons fresh onion juice
2 cups vegetable oil
1 tablespoon poppy seeds

In a blender, combine sugar, mustard, salt, vinegar and onion juice; blend thoroughly. With blender running, slowly stream in oil; continue blending until dressing emulsifies. Turn off blender and fold in poppy seeds. Transfer Poppy Seed Dressing to an airtight container and refrigerate up to 3 weeks. Serve over any kind of fruit salad.

Restaurant Recipe

Chickanellas

5550 Highway 59 North
Grove, OK 74344
918-787-5275
Find us on Facebook

Chickanellas is a fun, funky, quaint little eatery and Grove's newest breakfast and lunch hot spot. A variety of tasty choices are available, such as healthy wraps, sandwiches, salads, quiche, and homemade soups. Chickanellas also accommodates diners who are vegetarian and gluten-free or who have food allergies. In addition to breakfast and lunch, the eatery also offers many delicious desserts to satisfy your sweet tooth. Need a pick-me-up? Guests can also enjoy espresso drinks, lattes, cappuccinos, and frappés. At Chickanellas, you never know what new specials might be offered or new menu items might be added. Stop by for homemade food and friendly service.

Daily: 8:00 am to 2:00 pm

Aunt Kay's Carrot Cake

2 cups sugar
2 cups flour
2 teaspoons baking soda
2 teaspoons ground cinnamon
1 teaspoon salt
1½ cups vegetable oil
4 eggs
3 cups shredded carrots

Preheat oven to 350°. In a large bowl, whisk together sugar, flour, baking soda, cinnamon and salt. Mix in oil and eggs, then fold in carrots. Divide batter between 2 (9-inch) round floured, greased cake pans. Bake 40 minutes or until a toothpick inserted into center comes out clean.

Cream Cheese Frosting:

1 (8-ounce) package cream cheese, softened
½ cup butter, softened
1 teaspoon vanilla extract
3 cups powdered sugar

In a large bowl, combine cream cheese and butter; with a handheld electric mixer set to medium speed, beat together cream cheese and butter until smooth. Add vanilla and beat until combined. Add powdered sugar ½ cup at a time, beating into mixture until completely combined and smooth. Assemble cake, applying frosting between layers and over entire cake. Enjoy.

Restaurant Recipe

Monster Cookies

12 eggs
2 pounds brown sugar
4 cups white sugar
3 teaspoons vanilla extract
3 teaspoons light Karo syrup
1 pound chocolate chips
8 teaspoons baking soda
3 pounds peanut butter
18 cups old-fashioned oats
1 pound M&M's candy
1 pound butter

Preheat oven to 350°. In a large stand mixer fitted with a paddle attachment, combine ingredients in the order listed, mixing thoroughly after each addition. Using an ice cream scoop, drop mounds of dough several inches apart on a greased baking sheet; with scoop, indent each mound in the center. Bake 10 to 12 minutes; cool on baking sheet before enjoying. Makes 80 cookies.

Restaurant Recipe

1909

4 West 3rd Street
Grove, OK 74344
918-801-7518
www.1909grove.com • Find us on Facebook

If you're looking for somewhere fun, look no further than Grove's gastropub, 1909. The team at 1909 specializes in scratch-made American food and craft beer. The menu has a variety of options, ranging from pub-style foods, such as nachos, wings, and cheese curds, to high-end steaks and salmon. Inside, you'll also find Blue Duck Brew House, a full-service bar featuring ten Oklahoma craft beers on tap and an espresso machine serving Oklahoma-roasted coffee. Stop by for your morning coffee, your evening beverage, or, better yet, both. At 1909 and Blue Duck Brew House, there is something for everyone.

Wednesday & Thursday: 11:00 am to 9:00 pm
Friday & Saturday: 11:00 am to 10:00 pm

Slow-Cooker Pot Stew

2 cups diced carrot
½ cup diced celery
½ cup diced onion
2 cups diced potatoes
1 (2 pound) chuck roast
Seasoned salt to taste
Salt and pepper to taste

Combine carrot, celery, onion and potatoes in bottom of slow cooker. Trim most of the fat from roast; season with seasoned salt and salt and pepper. Place roast on top of vegetables. Do not add any liquids. Natural juices from the vegetables and meat are enough. Cook on low for 8 hours or until done.

Local Favorite

Luscious Potato Casserole

2 cups cottage cheese
1 cup sour cream
⅓ cup sliced green onions
1 clove garlic, minced
2 teaspoons salt
5 cups cubed cooked potatoes
½ cup shredded Cheddar cheese
Paprika as needed

Preheat oven to 350°. In a large bowl, combine cottage cheese, sour cream, green onion, garlic and salt. Fold in potatoes. Pour into a greased 1.5-quart casserole dish, top with cheese and sprinkle with paprika. Bake 40 minutes.

Local Favorite

Local Flavor

206 East Franklin Street
Haskell, OK 74436
918-482-4749
Find us on Facebook

Michelle Brashear grew up in the small town of Haskell. Her love for home cooking came from her Grandma Ada. Michelle has always loved to cook for her family and friends. It's her way of showing she cares. After years of hearing she should open a restaurant, Michelle and her husband, Greg, purchased a building that once housed an antique

store built by her sixth-grade teacher's family. Through a lot of blood, sweat, tears, and prayers, the Brashears opened Local Flavor in November 2017, a dream of Michelle's since she was a child. Come have a meal with Michelle and her family, and she'll make you feel right at home.

Tuesday – Saturday: 11:00 am to 8:30 pm
Sunday: 11:00 am to 3:00 pm

Chicken Salad Sandwiches

5 pounds chicken breast fillets
1 stick butter
Salt and pepper to taste
2 cups mayonnaise
1 red onion, diced
1 cup dill relish
2 cups halved cherry tomatoes
1½ to 2 tablespoons Dijon mustard
¼ cup sugar
Texas toast (or croissants) for serving

In a slow cooker, combine chicken, butter and salt and pepper; add water to cover and cook 6 hours or until chicken pulls apart with a fork. Remove chicken from slow cooker, reserving stock. When chicken has cooled, shred with a fork and transfer to a large bowl. Mix in mayonnaise, onion, relish, tomatoes, mustard, sugar and salt and pepper. Stir in reserved stock, 1 tablespoon at a time, until mixture reaches desired consistency. Serve between 2 slices Texas toast or inside sliced croissants.

Restaurant Recipe

Buffalo Chip Cookies

4 sticks butter, softened
2 cups packed brown sugar
2 cups white sugar
1 tablespoon vanilla extract
4 cups all-purpose flour
2 teaspoons baking soda
2 teaspoons baking powder
1 teaspoon salt
1 (12-ounce) package milk
chocolate chips
1 cup old-fashioned oats
1 cup cornflakes cereal
1 cup shredded coconut
1 cup chopped nuts, optional

Preheat oven to 350°. In the bowl of a stand mixer fitted with a paddle attachment, cream together butter, brown sugar, white sugar and vanilla until light and fluffy. In another bowl, whisk together flour, baking soda, baking powder and salt; fold into creamed mixture. Fold in chocolate chips, oats, cornflakes, coconut and nuts. Drop by spoonfuls 1½-inch apart. Bake 10 to 11 minutes or until edges are just browned. Cool before eating.

Restaurant Recipe

Rustler's BBQ

806 East Industry Road
Henryetta, OK 74437
918-650-9800
Find us on Facebook

Rustler's BBQ is a small-town barbecue joint that is owned and operated by Henryetta native Steve Sanford and his wife, Melinda Sanford. Rustler's offers southern barbecue with a twist as well as impeccable facilities and service. The restaurant believes in excellence, so all of their meat is slow smoked over locally sourced pecan wood in a rotisserie-style smoker for the best flavor. Rustler's takes pride in the quality of its food and its excellent customer service. Come see why KOCO 5 viewers voted Rustler's BBQ one of the top five barbecue spots in Oklahoma.

Thursday – Sunday: 11:00 am to 9:00 pm

Rustler's Borrachos Beans

1 pound bacon, cubed
1 onion, diced
1 stick butter
1 (32-ounce) carton chicken stock
1 (2-pound) package pinto beans, rinsed
and drained
1 tablespoon Cajun seasoning
1 (10-ounce) can Rotel tomatoes with
green chiles, lime and cilantro
1 (12-ounce) can Coors beer
1 tablespoon salt
½ tablespoon pepper
1 tablespoon garlic and herb seasoning

In a large stockpot over medium-high heat, fry bacon and onion in butter. When bacon is crisp and onion is translucent, add remaining ingredients to pot. Add water as needed to cover beans. Bring to a boil, then reduce to medium-low heat; simmer 2 to 3 hours or until beans are tender, adding water as needed.

Restaurant Recipe

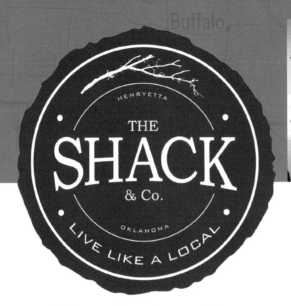

The Shack & Co.

509 West Main Street
Henryetta, OK 74437
918-652-9809
Find us on Facebook

Opened in June 2016 by Amanda and Whitney Weimer, The Shack & Co. is a locally owned eatery with one mission in mind: to provide fresh, quality products to the Henryetta community. The couple puts a local spin on creative, healthy food in a unique way. At The Shack & Co., you'll find delicious sandwiches and refreshing salads, two staples that have made the eatery a neighborhood favorite since it opened. You can also enjoy house-made paninis and flatbread pizzas. Whether you're a carnivore, a vegetarian, or a vegan, there's something for everyone. Drop by The Shack & Co. today and live like a local.

Tuesday – Friday: 10:00 am to 2:00 pm

The Cali

2 slices sourdough bread
1 to 2 tablespoons cream cheese
½ avocado, pitted and sliced
Salt and pepper to taste
1 to 2 slices peppered turkey
1 slice pepper Jack cheese
¼ cup raw spinach

On one slice bread, spread cream cheese; on the other slice, layer avocado slices and season with salt and pepper. Layer turkey, cheese and spinach over avocado; press sandwich together. Toast on a panini press until cheese is melted and bread is crisp.

Restaurant Recipe

Cream Cheese Brownies

4 ounces cream cheese, softened
½ cup sour cream
1 cup plus 2 tablespoons sugar, divided
⅔ cup plus 1 tablespoon all-purpose flour, divided
½ teaspoon baking powder
½ teaspoon salt
4 ounces semisweet baking chocolate
1 stick unsalted butter
2 eggs
1 teaspoon vanilla extract

Preheat oven to 325°. Spray an 8-inch square baking pan with nonstick spray and line with parchment paper; set aside. In a bowl, beat together cream cheese and sour cream with a handheld electric mixer; beat in 2 tablespoons sugar and 1 tablespoon flour, then set aside. In a large bowl, combine ⅔ remaining flour, baking powder and salt; set aside. In a microwave-safe bowl, microwave chocolate and butter in 30-second intervals, stirring each time, until smooth. In another bowl, combine remaining 1 cup sugar, eggs and vanilla; stir in melted chocolate, then stir in flour mixture. Spread half of brownie batter in bottom of prepared baking pan. Spread cream cheese mixture over top of brownie batter. Drizzle remaining brownie batter over cream cheese layer. Bake 45 minutes. Cool before cutting. Enjoy.

Restaurant Recipe

Esperance Bakery

610 West Main Street
Jenks, OK 74037
918-528-6544
www.esperancebakery.com
Find us on Facebook

Esperance Bakery offers its valued customers fresh-made baked goods, including handmade croissants, jelly rolls, pastries, and more. Esperance uses high-quality local ingredients, like organic flour, butter, sugar, milk, and cream, to craft handmade pastries. These minimally processed ingredients allow the bakery to create delicacies such as its specialty croissant dough stuffed with a variety of fillings, from ham and cheese to chocolate. The tasty treats combined with exceptional service make Esperance Bakery the perfect place to find a quick pick-me-up.

Tuesday – Friday: 6:30 am to 2:00 pm
Saturday: 7:30 am to noon

Homemade Lemon Curd

This tasty lemon curd can be baked into the Tart Crust or enjoyed on anything that goes well with delicious lemon.

¾ cup organic lemon juice
¾ cup organic sugar
3 eggs
1 stick unsalted butter, sliced into tablespoons

In a small saucepan, whisk together lemon juice, sugar and eggs; place over medium-low heat and whisk constantly until mixture begins to thicken. Whisk in 1 tablespoon butter at a time until incorporated. Pour Lemon Curd into a dish and cover with plastic wrap, pushing down to ensure plastic wrap makes contact with surface of curd (this will prevent a skin from forming on curd). Refrigerate until ready to use.

Restaurant Recipe

Frangipani

¾ cup chopped almonds
1 stick unsalted butter, softened
¾ cup sugar
1 tablespoon almond extract
3 tablespoons Myers's dark rum
3 tablespoons all-purpose flour
1 egg
1 (9- to 10-inch) premade
unbaked Tart Crust
Fruit of choice for topping (fresh berries,
poached pears, etc.)

In a bowl, mix together almonds, butter, sugar, almond extract, rum, flour and egg, forming what is almost a paste. Fill Tart Crust with Frangipani and top with fruit. Bake at 350° for about 40 minutes or until filling is only slightly jiggly.

Restaurant Recipe

Tart Crust

1 large egg yolk
1 teaspoon vanilla extract
1⅓ cups all-purpose flour
⅓ cup sugar
1 stick cold butter, cut into ¼-inch cubes

In a small bowl, whisk together egg yolk and vanilla with 2 teaspoons water; set aside. In a medium bowl, whisk together flour and sugar; add butter a little at a time until incorporated, pinching and mixing until mixture resembles coarse crumbs. Add egg mixture, mixing with hands until a firm dough forms. Press dough into a lightly greased 9- to 10-inch tart pan or multiple 3- to 4-inch tartlet pans. Using a fork, poke small holes over entire crust, then refrigerate until ready to bake. For fillings that don't require additional baking (like Lemon Curd), blind-bake crust at 350° for 8 to 10 minutes, then cool and fill. Otherwise, add filling and bake per fillings requirements. Enjoy.

Restaurant Recipe

Waterfront GRILL

120 Aquarium Drive
Jenks, OK 74037
918-518-6300
www.waterfrontgrilljenks.com • Find us on Facebook

The Waterfront Grill , conceived and operated by the Blacketer family, opened in the spring of 2011. It all started with a commitment to using fresh fish and, later, great steaks. But the Waterfront Grill is so much more than a seafood and steak restaurant. It also serves delicious burgers, sandwiches, sushi, salads, and a fabulous weekend brunch. Guests will also enjoy a very special bar scene featuring award-winning cucumber martinis, signature wines, and draft beers. Drop by for brunch, enjoy lively jazz music, visit the omelet station, or build your own Bloody Mary. Whatever you decide, you're sure to find something tasty at Waterfront Grill.

Monday – Thursday: 11:00 am to 9:00 pm
Friday: 11:00 am to 10:00 pm
Saturday: 10:00 am to 10:00 pm
Sunday: 10:00 am to 9:00 pm

Salmon Patties

1 (16-ounce) can pink salmon, drained
2 eggs, beaten
16 saltine crackers, crushed
Salt to taste
Pepper to taste
½ teaspoon baking powder
1 cup all-purpose flour
Vegetable oil for frying

Mix together salmon, eggs, crackers, salt, pepper and baking powder in a bowl. Form mixture into 3-inch patties that are ½ inch thick. Coat with flour; set aside. Heat ½-inch of oil in a skillet over medium heat. Place patties in oil and fry until golden brown, flipping once.

Local Favorite

Spicy Grilled Potatoes

4 baking potatoes
1 cup Italian salad dressing
1 teaspoon salt
¼ teaspoon pepper

Preheat oven to 400°. Wash potatoes well. Pat dry, then place on a baking sheet. Bake potatoes 30 minutes. While potatoes are still hot, slice diagonally in ½-inch-thick slices; place in a shallow baking dish. Pour dressing over potatoes and let stand 1 hour. Remove potatoes and place on grill, 3 to 4 inches from hot coals. Grill 8 to 10 minutes on each side until brown. Season with salt and pepper.

Local Favorite

The Artichoke

35878 South Highway 82
Langley, OK 74350
918-782-9855
www.theartichokeatgrand.com • Find us on Facebook

Since 2004, The Artichoke has served award-winning American cuisine in the Grand Lake area. At The Artichoke, you will find mouthwatering steaks, fresh seafood, chicken and pasta dishes, handcrafted salads, nightly specials, and more. The restaurant uses only the freshest ingredients sourced from local growers and producers, so you'll get the freshest plate every visit. The restaurant is located inside a century-old farmhouse, providing you a cozy, casual atmosphere in which to greet old friends and meet new friends while enjoying the finest dining. The Artichoke also boasts a full-service bar with an excellent wine list. Come see why The Artichoke is one of the Grand Lake area's top-rated restaurants.

Tuesday – Thursday: 5:00 pm to 8:00 pm
Friday & Saturday: 5:00 pm to 8:30 pm

Scampi Sauté

8 tablespoons scampi butter
6 freshly frozen extra jumbo shrimp
2½ ounces sliced mushrooms
1 tablespoon chopped shallot
1 endive, roasted
1 lemon wedge

In a skillet over medium heat, melt scampi butter. Add shrimp and sauté 4 minutes or until pink and cooked through. Add mushrooms and shallot and stir. Partially drain butter so that shrimp are not floating in butter. Serve in a scampi boat with an endive and a lemon wedge.

Restaurant Recipe

Tartar Sauce

2 tablespoons Creole mustard
1 tablespoon tarragon wine vinegar
Tabasco sauce to taste
Salt and pepper to taste
1 cup olive oil
1 tablespoon paprika
½ cup chopped celery
1 cup chopped green onion
1 teaspoon chopped garlic
½ cup chopped fresh parsley
2 tablespoons horseradish
2 tablespoons anchovy paste
⅛ teaspoon cayenne pepper
2 tablespoons lemon juice

In a large mixing bowl, combine mustard and vinegar. Whisk in Tabasco and salt and pepper. Continue whisking vigorously while gradually adding oil. Stir in remaining ingredients until incorporated. Enjoy.

Restaurant Recipe

Country Cottage Restaurant

6570 Highway 82 South
Locust Grove, OK 74352
918-479-6439
Find us on Facebook

Established in 1986, Country Cottage Restaurant is a family-owned restaurant that has decades of history in the Locust Grove area. Family is at the core of Country Cottage Restaurant, from the dishes made with delicious recipes passed down through generations to the hometown hospitality you receive tableside. There is nothing better than sharing a meal and a table with people you love, and at Country Cottage Restaurant, getting together with family and friends for a homemade meal is easy. Settle in to a home-style buffet featuring hand-breaded chicken-fried steak, fried chicken, homemade pies, tasty cobblers, and much more. Come see why Country Cottage Restaurant has so many loyal customers.

Tuesday – Thursday: 11:00 am to 8:00 pm
Friday: 11:00 am to 8:30 pm
Saturday: 7:30 am to 8:30 pm
Sunday: 7:30 am to 3:30 pm

Mock "Pecan" Pie

3 eggs, beaten
½ cup white sugar
⅔ cup packed brown sugar
1 teaspoon vanilla extract
⅓ cup melted butter
⅔ cup rolled oats
⅔ cup shredded coconut
1 (9-inch) frozen deep-dish pie
crust, thawed

Preheat oven to 350°. In a medium bowl, combine eggs, white sugar and brown sugar; beat well. Stir in vanilla and butter, mixing thoroughly. Fold in oats and coconut. Pour mixture into pie crust, then bake 30 minutes. Cool before serving.

Restaurant Recipe

Corn Muffins

2 cups white cornmeal
2 cups all-purpose flour
½ tablespoon baking soda
1 teaspoon salt
1 cup sugar
2 sticks butter, melted
2 cups buttermilk
4 eggs

Preheat oven to 350°. In a bowl, whisk together cornmeal, flour, baking soda and salt. In another bowl, whisk sugar into butter until dissolved; whisk in buttermilk and eggs. Combine wet and dry mixtures, taking care not to overmix. Pour mixture into greased muffin pans, then bake 20 minutes or until a toothpick inserted into the center of a muffin comes out clean.

Restaurant Recipe

Gino's Italian Ristorante

139 West Shawnee Street
Muskogee, OK 74403
918-686-7773
www.ginosmuskogee.com • Find us on Facebook

Benvenuto a Gino's Italian Ristorante! This restaurant and pizzeria serves Italian fare done right—fresh, fast, and affordable. At Gino's, you'll discover Italian staples like baked ziti, eggplant parmigiana, manicotti, stromboli, lasagna, and so much more. Also, you can't go wrong with one of Gino's specialty personal pizzas, made fresh with your toppings of choice, from black olives and Canadian bacon to pepperoni and pineapple. Be sure to finish your meal with a selection from the dessert menu. Try the tiramisu, Italy's most famous dessert. It's clear to anyone who visits that the team at Gino's Italian Ristorante is passionate about preparing great food for their valued guests.

Tuesday – Sunday: 11:00 am to 9:30 pm

Chicken Bites

8 boneless, skinless chicken breast halves
1½ cups buttermilk
1 (1-ounce) package ranch dressing mix
2 cups flour
Salt and pepper to taste
Oil for frying

Cut chicken into bite-size pieces; place in a resealable bowl. In another bowl, combine buttermilk and ranch dressing mix; pour over chicken, seal and refrigerate overnight. In another bowl, mix together flour and salt and pepper. Preheat oil to 350° in a saucepan over medium heat. Dip chicken in flour mixture and drop into preheated oil; fry 6 to 7 minutes or until golden brown.

Local Favorite

Buttermilk Biscuits

2 cups all-purpose flour
¼ teaspoon baking soda
2 teaspoons baking powder
2 teaspoons salt
¼ cup vegetable shortening
1 cup buttermilk

Preheat oven 450°. Grease bottom of a 9x13-inch pan; place in oven to preheat. In a bowl, sift together flour, baking soda, baking powder and salt. Cut shortening into flour mixture until crumbled. Add buttermilk; mix just until combined. Drop dough in large spoonfuls into preheated pan. Bake 20 minutes or until golden brown. Makes about 12 biscuits.

Local Favorite

Harmony House

208 South 7th Street
Muskogee, OK 74401
918-687-8653
www.harmonyhouse4lunch.com
Find us on Facebook

Harmony House is a café and bakery housed in a 100-year-old home in the heart of downtown Muskogee. The restaurant offers a lunch menu with options ranging from burgers and sandwiches to soups and salads. Guests can also order the daily special, which always includes dessert. Providing the freshest food to its customers is Harmony House's goal. That's why the restaurant begins every morning by scratch-baking its hamburger buns, clover rolls, cinnamon rolls, and other bakery selections. In fact, the bakery at Harmony House has been creating traditional baked goods for more than twenty-six years. Come see why Harmony House was voted Muskogee's best place for lunch.

Lunch:
Monday – Saturday: 11:00 am to 2:30 pm
Bakery:
Monday – Friday: 9:00 am to 5:00 pm
Saturday: 9:00 am to 3:00 pm

Toll House Pie

2 eggs
½ cup all-purpose flour
½ cup white sugar
½ cup packed brown sugar
¾ cup butter
1 cup chopped nuts
1 cup chocolate chips
1 (9-inch) frozen pie crust, thawed

Preheat oven to 350°. To a mixing bowl, add eggs; with a handheld electric mixer, beat eggs on high until foamy. Mix in remaining ingredients until well combined. Pour filling into pie crust. Bake 1 hour until crust is browned and filling is set.

Restaurant Recipe

Runt's Bar-B-Que & Grill

3003 West Okmulgee Avenue
Muskogee, OK 74401
918-681-3900
runtsbarbq.com • Find us on Facebook

Runt's Bar-B-Que is a family-owned business run by Russell Pratt. After spending more than fifteen years working in the restaurant industry, Pratt opened Runt's Bar-B-Que & Grill in 2001. With the help of his family, Pratt has made Runt's a Muskogee staple where everyone loves to eat, locals and visitors alike. Everything served is made from scratch or prepared from the finest available ingredients, from the house-made barbecue sauce to the banana pudding to the delicious slow-smoked pork spare ribs. Give Runt's a try when you visit Muskogee. You won't be disappointed.

Tuesday – Saturday: 11:00 am to 9:00 pm

Hot Breakfast Rolls

½ cup melted margarine

½ cup packed brown sugar

1 (3.5-ounce) package cook-and-serve butterscotch pudding mix

1 teaspoon ground cinnamon

Nuts or raisins to taste

1 (24-count) package frozen Parker House–style rolls

In a bowl, whisk together margarine, brown sugar, pudding mix and cinnamon. Arrange rolls in a greased Bundt pan; pour mixture over rolls. Add nuts and raisins. Cover with a damp cloth; let rise overnight at room temperature. Bake at 400° for 15 to 20 minutes.

Local Favorite

Reuben Casserole

1 (12-ounce) can corned beef

1 (16-ounce) can sauerkraut, drained

2 cups shredded Swiss cheese

½ cup Thousand Island dressing

1 large tomato, sliced

1 cup pumpernickel breadcrumbs

2 tablespoons margarine

Salt and pepper to taste

2 tablespoons caraway seeds

Preheat oven to 350°. In a lightly greased 2-quart casserole dish, layer each ingredient in order, starting with corned beef and ending with caraway seeds. Bake 30 minutes. Rest 5 minutes before serving.

Local Favorite

The Lokal Okmulgee

212 East 6th Street
Okmulgee, OK 74447
918-938-0600
Find us on Facebook

Opened in 2017, The Lokal Okmulgee is a coffeehouse with a goal: to provide the Okmulgee community something out of the norm with Lokal flair. The freshly baked muffins and bagels and house-made yogurt parfaits pair perfectly with the Oklahoma-roasted coffee. Stopping in for lunch? You'll love The Lokal's fresh salads, sandwiches, and soups, like the spicy chicken tortilla soup. Every item is unique and made to order, so you get a one-of-a-kind, fresh dining experience every time. Don't forget to pick up a signature drink to get your caffeine fix any time of the day. Whether it's the Lokal Macchiato or the White Bison made with Oklahoma-roasted eôté coffee beans, you will not be disappointed.

Monday – Friday: 7:00 am to 5:00 pm
Saturday: 7:00 am to 2:00 pm

Lemon Chicken

1 clove garlic, mashed
½ teaspoon salt
½ teaspoon pepper
½ teaspoon dried thyme
¼ cup olive oil
½ cup lemon juice
2 tablespoons grated onion
2 broiler chickens, halved

In a zip-close bag, mix together all ingredients except chickens. Add chickens and marinate several hours or overnight. Prepare grill, ensuring coals are white-hot. Remove chickens from marinade; place chickens on grill. Cook until done, brushing several times with remaining marinade.

Local Favorite

Brandied Fruit

1 (20-ounce) can peach slices, drained
1 (20-ounce) can pineapple
chunks, drained
1 (20-ounce) can apricot halves, drained
1 (20-ounce) can pear halves, drained
1 (18-ounce) jar apple rings, drained
½ stick butter
½ cup sugar
2 tablespoons flour
1 cup sherry

Place fruit in a 9x13-inch casserole dish. Using a double boiler over medium heat, cook butter, sugar, flour and sherry until thick; pour over fruit. Cover casserole dish and refrigerate overnight. Bake at 350° for 45 minutes. Serve warm.

Local Favorite

Click's Steakhouse

409 Harrison Street
Pawnee, OK 74058
918-762-2231
www.clickssteakhouse.com • Find us on Facebook

In 1962, Clifton "Click" Nelson opened Click's Alamo Club. He was known for his outstanding steaks and colorful language. Burgers and fries were served for lunch, but if a customer ordered them for dinner, Click would yell from the kitchen, "Who ordered the @!#?$% fries? They can go across the street to the @!#?$% Tastee Freeze for that!" It was common for locals to encourage newcomers to order fries just to watch their reaction to Click's tirade. Still, everyone knew Click's bark was worse than his bite. Since then, the restaurant has changed hands thrice. Though the building has undergone changes, the menu has expanded, and the name has changed, the quality of the steaks and the unique aging and preparation technique remains the same.

Tuesday – Thursday: 11:00 am to 8:00 pm
Friday & Saturday: 11:00 am to 9:00 pm
Sunday: 11:00 am to 2:00 pm

Potato Casserole

1 (30-ounce) package shredded hash brown potatoes, thawed
1 cup cream of chicken soup
1 (16-ounce) package sour cream
2 cups shredded Cheddar cheese
1 teaspoon salt
1 cup chopped onion
2 cups crumbled potato chips
1 stick butter, melted

Preheat oven to 375°. In a large bowl, combine hash browns, soup, sour cream, cheese, salt and onion; mix until well combined, then transfer to a greased casserole dish. Evenly spread chips over top and drizzle melted butter over everything. Bake 45 minutes to 1 hour or until browned.

Family Favorite

Tollhouse Pie

6 sticks butter, melted
12 eggs, beaten
2 cups white sugar
1 (16-ounce) package light brown sugar
2 cups all-purpose flour
5 cups chocolate chips
5 cups chopped pecans
4 (9-inch) frozen deep-dish pie crusts, thawed

Preheat oven to 350°. To a large mixing bowl, add butter. Whisk in eggs and white sugar, then add remaining ingredients; mix well. Divide filling between pie crusts and bake 48 minutes or until golden brown.

Restaurant Recipe

Garrett Wrangler

421 South 14th Street
Ponca City, OK 74601
580-767-8880
Find us on Facebook

Garrett Wrangler is a country-style restaurant serving up down-home fare that is good for the soul. The restaurant serves an all-day breakfast, featuring classic breakfast items like omelets, sausage, hash browns, bacon, pancakes, and more. If you'd prefer a later start, stop by for lunch and sample country-fried steak sandwiches, BLTs, and specialty burgers. For dinner, you can also dine on pork chops, chicken strips, country-fried steak, chicken-fried chicken, and so much more. Don't forget dessert, like soda floats, pies, sundaes, fried cookie dough, cinnamon rolls, and muffins. No matter what you're hankerin' for, Garrett Wrangler has got you covered.

Daily: 6:00 am to 9:00 pm

Banana Mallow Pie

1 (3.4-ounce) box instant
vanilla pudding
1¾ cups milk
1½ cups miniature marshmallows
1 cup whipped cream
2 bananas, sliced into coins
1 (9-inch) graham cracker pie crust

Combine pudding and milk; refrigerate until chilled. Fold in marshmallows and whipped cream. Arrange banana slices in bottom of pie crust. Pour filling over top of bananas. Place in refrigerator several hours (or overnight) before serving.

Local Favorite

Ground Sirloin Dinner

2 pounds ground sirloin
7 to 8 potatoes, peeled and sliced
3 to 4 onions, sliced
1 (10.75-ounce) can cream of
chicken soup
Salt and pepper to taste

Preheat oven to 350°. Form sirloin into patties and place in single layer in bottom of a casserole dish. Alternate sliced potatoes with sliced onions in layers over meat. Pour soup and 1 soup can of water over top and sprinkle with salt and pepper. Bake 1 hour.

Local Favorite

Rusty Barrell Supper Club

2005 North 14th Street
Ponca City, OK 74601
580-765-6689
www.rustybarrellsupperclub.com • Find us on Facebook

For more than forty years, Bill and Judy Coddington proudly operated the Rusty Barrell Supper Club, serving folks from all fifty states and ninety countries. Today, the tradition continues with their son Rick Hancock and his wife, Kim, who run the restaurant as it has been since 1974. This American steakhouse serves the finest beef, aged a minimum of twenty-eight days to ensure ultimate tenderness and taste. All entrées are served with the famous salad bar, a baked potato, and freshly baked bread. The Rusty Barrell's goal is to exceed their customers' expectations every visit by offering the finest steaks and friendliest service in the warmest atmosphere.

"From our family to yours; God bless!"

Lunch:
Tuesday – Friday: 11:00 am to 1:30 pm
Dinner:
Tuesday – Thursday: 5:00 pm to 9:30 pm
Friday & Saturday: 5:00 pm to 10:00 pm

Potato Salad

2 cups mayonnaise
1 cup mustard
1 cup chopped green onion
1 cup chopped red bell pepper
1 cup whole-kernel corn
½ cup chopped red onion
3 tablespoons hot sauce
3 tablespoons kosher salt
3 tablespoons pepper
1 tablespoon paprika
½ lemon, juiced
5 pounds potatoes, boiled and diced

In a bowl, combine all ingredients except potatoes; whisk until well combined. Fold in potatoes until fully incorporated. Chill several hours before serving.

Restaurant Recipe

Sautéed Mushrooms

1 pound European-style butter blend
2½ pounds fresh mushrooms, washed
10 sprigs fresh thyme, stems removed
2 tablespoons kosher salt
1 tablespoon pepper
1 tablespoon minced garlic
1 tablespoon soy sauce

In a deep skillet over low heat, melt butter; cook 5 minutes or until butter browns, swirling the skillet every minute or so. Add mushrooms, thyme, salt, pepper and garlic; sauté 8 to 10 minutes. Once mushrooms are soft and lightly caramelized, add soy sauce. Toss, then transfer to a slow cooker and hold on low heat until ready to serve.

Restaurant Recipe

7C Land & Cattle Steakhouse

7500 US Highway 177
Red Rock, OK 74651
580-723-1060
www.sevenclans.com • Find us on Facebook

The 7C Land & Cattle Steakhouse is a casual fine-dining steakhouse that features the finest certified Angus beef steaks, seafood and shellfish, and regional specialties. In addition to entrées, you'll also enjoy an extensive assortment of appetizers, salads, side dishes, and desserts. The steakhouse can accommodate ninety-eight diners at once: sixty-seven in the dining room, twenty on the outdoor patio, and eleven at the U-shaped bar. You'll always have a seat at the table when you visit. The atmosphere brings the experience together with solid wood tabletops, comfortable leather seats, large chandeliers, a metal-topped bar, and LED accent lighting. Visit 7C Land & Cattle Steakhouse, a cut above the rest.

Monday – Saturday: 11:00 am to 10:00 pm

Garlic Butter

2 sticks salted butter, softened
2 tablespoons chopped fresh parsley
2 tablespoons chopped green onion
2 tablespoons minced garlic
Dash lemon juice
Pepper to taste

In a mixing bowl, combine all ingredients and mix until smooth and well combined. Use immediately or refrigerate in an airtight container up to 2 weeks.

Restaurant Recipe

House Seasoning

1 cup coarse sea salt
¼ cup granulated garlic
¼ cup pepper

In a bowl, whisk together all ingredients until evenly distributed. This is the perfect all-purpose seasoning for a variety of meats and side dishes. Try on beef, chicken, fish and more.

Restaurant Recipe

Salmon Dill Relish

1 cup diced tomato, seeds removed
2 tablespoons diced red onion
1 tablespoon diced red bell pepper
1 tablespoon diced green bell pepper
1 teaspoon lemon juice
1½ teaspoons chopped fresh dill
Salt and pepper to taste

In a mixing bowl, combine all ingredients. Gently fold together until well combined. Serve over cooked salmon.

Restaurant Recipe

Vidalia's Café

319 North Muskogee Avenue
Tahlequah, OK 74464
918-456-5551
Find us on Facebook

Craving an all-American meal? Look no further than Vidalia's Café, serving up tasty classics that will keep you coming back. Take your pick of a variety of house-made sandwiches, including clubs, BLTs, and classic Monte Cristos. Vidalia's also offers a selection of old-time favorites, such as tamales, nachos, coneys, and chili. If you want something a bit lighter, you might also try a house-made salad, like the Henderson, served with turkey, bacon, Cheddar, tomatoes, iceberg lettuce, and croutons. Don't forget to try a homemade dressing with your salad or pick up a slice of pie or cake for dessert. Whatever you're in the mood for, Vidalia's has you covered.

Monday – Friday: 11:00 am to 7:00 pm
Saturday: 11:00 am to 3:00 pm

Strawberry Cake

If you like lemon cakes, you can use lemon Jell-O in place of strawberry Jell-O and lemon zest in place of strawberries.

1 box white cake mix
1 (3-ounce) box strawberry Jell-O
½ cup butter, softened
½ cup shortening
½ cup water
3 tablespoons flour, plus more as needed
4 eggs
1 teaspoon vanilla extract
¾ cup sliced fresh strawberries

Preheat oven to 350°. In a large bowl, mix together all ingredients except strawberries. Toss strawberries in flour, then fold into batter. Bake 42 minutes or until a toothpick inserted into center comes out clean.

Restaurant Recipe

Vidalia's Famous Cheesecake

1 cup graham cracker crumbs
3 tablespoons plus 1 cup sugar, divided
3 tablespoons unsalted butter, melted
4 (8-ounce) packages cream cheese, softened
1 cup sour cream
1 teaspoon vanilla extract
4 eggs

Preheat oven to 325°. In a bowl, mix together graham cracker crumbs, 3 tablespoons sugar and butter; press into bottom of a 9-inch springform baking pan. Bake crust 10 minutes, then cool. In a bowl, beat cream cheese with a handheld electric mixer until creamy. Add remaining 1 cup sugar and mix well. Blend in sour cream and vanilla. Beat in eggs 1 at a time. When completely combined, pour mixture into springform pan and bake 1 hour. Cool completely before removing from pan.

Restaurant Recipe

1924 Riverside Drive
Tulsa, OK 74119
918-582-4600
www.bluerosecafetulsa.com
Find us on Facebook

Welcome to Blue Rose Café. Surrounded by windows, roll-up garage doors, and a large patio area that overlooks the Arkansas River, Blue Rose Café is the best place in Tulsa to kick back and relax. The casual dining menu offers something for everyone. Customer favorites include the Blue Rose famous cheese fries and the blackened chicken. You can also enjoy tap beers, bottled imports and domestics, a wonderful wine selection, and custom cocktails. Whether you're looking for a quiet riverside dinner or a private party on the lower deck, you'll always enjoy fresh food, cold beer, enthusiastic service, and the best live music at Blue Rose Café.

Daily: 11:00 am to 10:00 pm

Oklahoma Grits

1½ cups dry quick grits

¾ cup butter

1 pound processed cheese, cubed

2 teaspoons seasoned salt

1 tablespoon Worcestershire sauce

½ teaspoon hot pepper sauce

2 teaspoons salt

3 eggs, beaten

Preheat oven to 350°. Lightly grease a 9x13-inch baking dish. In a medium saucepan, bring 6 cups water to a boil. Stir in grits and reduce heat to low; cover and cook 5 to 6 minutes, stirring occasionally. Mix in butter, cheese, seasoned salt, Worcestershire, hot pepper sauce and salt. Continue cooking 5 minutes or until cheese is melted. Remove from heat, cool slightly and fold in eggs. Pour into prepared baking dish. Bake 1 hour or until the top is lightly browned.

Local Favorite

Barbecue Carnitas

2 tablespoons tomato paste

2 tablespoons chipotle sauce (or adobo sauce)

3 cloves garlic

1 tablespoon all-purpose seasoning

1 Boston butt pork roast, cut into 2-inch pieces

1 cup beer (or chicken stock)

Tortillas for serving

Combine tomato paste, chipotle sauce, garlic and seasoning in a 5-quart slow cooker. Stir in pieces of pork roast. In a 2-cup glass measuring cup, microwave beer on high for 1½ to 2 minutes. Pour beer over pork roast. Do not stir. Cover and cook on high for 6 hours. Remove meat from the slow cooker; shred using 2 forks. For traditional carnitas, brown shredded pork in a skillet until the meat is crisp on the edges. Serve in flour or corn tortillas.

Local Favorite

Ike's Chili

1503 East 11th Street
Tulsa, OK 74115
918-838-9410
www.ikeschilius.com • Find us on Facebook

In 1908, Ike Johnson and his nephew Ivan Johnson opened Ike's Chili. Since then, the restaurant has been serving its famous chili to Tulsans and travelers alike. In the decades that followed its opening, Ike's Chili not only moved locations but also expanded to include sister locations. Over time, Ike's has remained true to its roots, preserving the same chili recipe that has kept guests coming back for over a century. Come taste the reason that, after all these years, Ike's chili is still considered the best chili in the city.

Monday – Friday: 10:00 am to 7:00 pm
Saturday: 10:00 am to 3:00 pm

Ike's Taco Burger

8 ounces ground beef

1 hamburger bun

2 leaves lettuce, chopped

Diced tomato and onion for topping

6 ounces Ike's chili (or chili of choice)

Grated Cheddar cheese, sliced jalapeños and ranch dressing for topping

Preheat broiler. Form beef into a patty and broil 3 to 4 inches from element, about 3 minutes; flip and broil other side until done. Meanwhile, toast bun. Place patty on bottom bun, then add lettuce, tomato and onion. Top with chili and cheese, jalapeños and ranch dressing. Top with top bun and enjoy.

Restaurant Recipe

Fritos Burrito

1 large flour tortilla

½ cup shredded lettuce

¼ cup diced tomato

¼ cup red beans

2 tablespoons sour cream

4 ounces Ike's chili (or chili of choice) plus more for topping

Grated Cheddar cheese, diced onion, sliced jalapeños, salsa and Fritos chips for topping

Warm tortilla on a griddle. Remove from griddle and add lettuce, tomato, beans and sour cream. Top with chili, then add cheese, onion, jalapeños, salsa and Fritos. Roll up tortilla, then add more chili and Cheddar. Enjoy.

Restaurant Recipe

Kilkenny's Irish Pub

1413 East 15th Street
Tulsa, OK 74120
918-582-8282
www.tulsairishpub.com
Find us on Facebook

Welcome to Kilkenny's Irish Pub, Tulsa's best destination for travelers and gathering place for friends. Combining his passion and talents together, owner Brett Rehorn opened this unique eatery in 2001. One of the nation's top-rated pubs, Kilkenny's boasts an extremely large menu as well as a varied selection of choice beverages. You'll enjoy an ever-changing monthly menu featuring authentic Irish dishes that can't be found anywhere else. With a wonderful atmosphere to match the food, you'll swear you've visited Éire itself. Stop by Kilkenny's Irish Pub and get a taste of Ireland without leaving Tulsa.

Monday – Friday: 11:00 am to 2:00 am
Saturday & Sunday: 9:00 am to 2:00 am

English Mustard Cream Sauce

1 tablespoon minced garlic
1 tablespoon minced shallot
2 sticks butter
1 cup all-purpose flour
1 quart chicken stock
¼ cup white wine
1 teaspoon salt
1 teaspoon pepper
2 cups heavy cream
4 tablespoons Colman's mustard

In a large saucepan over medium heat, sauté garlic and shallot in butter until soft. Stir in flour, cooking until mixture bubbles. Add chicken stock, wine, salt and pepper. Cook, stirring constantly, until sauce begins to thicken. Remove from heat and stir in heavy cream and mustard. Cool and store in refrigerator in an airtight container. Serve with Freshford Reuben Rolls. Makes 2 quarts.

Restaurant Recipe

Freshford Reuben Rolls

1 sheet filo dough
24 ounces corned beef
12 ounces sauerkraut
1 egg, beaten
Prepared English Mustard Cream
Sauce for dipping

Cut filo dough lengthwise into 12 (2½-inch) strips. Place 2 ounces corned beef on each, followed by 1 ounce sauerkraut. Roll up each filo strip and seal with a brush of egg. Arrange rolls on a baking sheet and bake at 350° for 8 minutes or until golden brown. Serve with prepared English Mustard Cream Sauce for dipping.

Restaurant Recipe

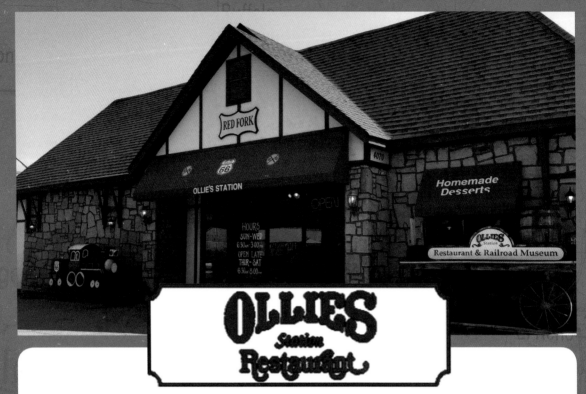

Ollie's Station Restaurant

4070 Southwest Boulevard
Tulsa, OK 74107
918-446-0524
www.olliesstation.com

People long for the food they remember eating while they were growing up. At Ollie's Station Restaurant, that's the kind of food you'll find: home-cooked favorites prepared and seasoned to perfection, just like Mom and Grandma used to make. Relax in the mom-and-pop atmosphere, enjoying the railroad motif while you dine. Ten model trains, from G-scale to Z-scale, run the length of the dining area, navigating through scale models of cities and towns. Railroad memorabilia adorn the walls and shelves. It is here—at the convergence of railroads, oil wells, and Route 66—that customers young and old come to experience heritage and a taste of traditional foods.

Sunday – Wednesday: 6:30 am to 3:00 pm
Thursday – Saturday: 6:30 am to 8:00 pm

Pasta Alfredo

6 ounces dry pasta of choice
3 teaspoons olive oil
½ tablespoon all-purpose flour
1 cup heavy cream
½ teaspoon salt
1 pinch pepper
½ teaspoon garlic powder
¼ cup shredded Parmesan cheese
¾ cup shredded Italian blend cheese

Bring a large saucepan of salted water to a boil; add pasta and cook per package directions to desired doneness. Drain pasta in colander. To a saucepan over low heat, add oil. Stir in flour until a smooth paste forms; cook 1 to 2 minutes to remove raw flour taste. Slowly whisk in heavy cream, breaking up any lumps of flour. Increase heat to medium-high and cook until sauce begins to thicken, about 2 minutes. Do not bring to a boil. Stir in salt, pepper and garlic powder. Remove from heat, then stir in Parmesan cheese and Italian blend cheese. Stir pasta into sauce and serve.

Restaurant Recipe

Smashed Potato Salad

1 cup mayonnaise
½ onion, diced
2 stalks celery, diced
½ cup vinegar
1 cup milk
1 tablespoon mustard
2 tablespoons cornstarch
4 tablespoons sugar
1½ tablespoons salt
½ teaspoon onion powder
2 teaspoons pepper
2 teaspoons celery seed
9 eggs, divided
6 to 7 potatoes, peeled, boiled and diced

Add mayonnaise, onion and celery to a large bowl; whisk together. In a large skillet over medium-low heat, combine vinegar, milk, mustard, cornstarch, sugar, salt, onion powder, pepper and celery seed; beat 1 egg and add to skillet. Cook until thickened, stirring occasionally; cool and add to bowl with mayonnaise mixture. In another skillet, scramble remaining 8 eggs; combine with mayonnaise mixture. Add potatoes to bowl; cover and refrigerate 1 hour. Mash mixture and stir to combine. Refrigerate until ready to serve.

Restaurant Recipe

The Restaurant at Gilcrease

1400 North Gilcrease Museum Road
Tulsa, OK 74127
918-596-2720
www.gilcrease.org • Find us on Facebook

The Restaurant at Gilcrease is located inside the Gilcrease Museum. Experience the breadth and depth of the museum's permanent collection as well as a variety of temporary exhibits that swap out every few months. When you've worked up an appetite, the Restaurant at Gilcrease will be waiting for you. Chef Lenny Borkowicz has prepared a menu featuring seasonal items with a touch of Southwest influence. Dine on classics like the Gilcrease Buffalo Burger, soups, salads, and pizza. If you stop by on Sunday, you can even enjoy a breakfast buffet that boasts waffle and omelet stations. Backdropped by the Osage Hills, food with a view is what they do.

Tuesday – Sunday: 11:00 am to 3:00 pm

Strawberry Vinaigrette

By executive chef Leonard Borkowicz.

1 pint fresh strawberries
2 tablespoons Dijon mustard
3 ounces honey
3 ounces apple cider vinegar
20 ounces salad oil
Salt and pepper to taste

Add strawberries, mustard, honey and vinegar to a blender. Blend until smooth. Slowly stream in oil while blender is running until the vinaigrette thickens. Add salt and pepper to taste and blend until combined. Enjoy.

Restaurant Recipe

Roosevelt's

1551 East 15th Street
Tulsa, OK 74120
918-591-2888
www.rooseveltstulsa.com • Find us on Facebook

Located in the heart of Cherry Street, Roosevelt's is a locally owned and family-operated gastropub. Roosevelt's proudly sources ingredients from local farms throughout the state of Oklahoma. The in-house bakery allows the pub to provide customers and other local restaurants with the freshest bread and house-made baked goods. Roosevelt's specializes in craft beer, offering eighty taps, but also provides a wine list curated by the very best sommeliers in town. You can also enjoy seasonal cocktails and a brunch menu that changes weekly. At Roosevelt's, you'll always find something new to excite your palate.

Sunday: 10:00 am to 10:00 pm
Monday – Thursday: 11:00 am to 11:00 pm
Friday: 11:00 am to 1:00 am
Saturday: 10:00 am to 1:00 am

Irene's Brownies

8 cups sugar
2 pounds butter
1 pound chocolate
12 eggs
4 teaspoons vanilla extract
1 teaspoon salt
4 cups self-rising flour

Cook at 300° for 1 hour. Top with homemade vanilla ice cream, house-made caramel and espresso crumbles.

Restaurant Recipe

the SPUDDER RESTAURANT

6536 East 50th Street
Tulsa, OK 74145
918-665-1416
www.thespudder.com • Find us on Facebook

John Phillips and John Brennemen opened The Spudder Restaurant in 1976. The restaurant is named after the cable tool rig, a 1920s-era piece of machinery used for drilling shallow wells, that is stationed outside. In 2011, Steve and Kim Jeffery bought The Spudder. Kim makes every dessert herself, and you'll love the buttery, flaky rolls that are served in an

old-style lunch box. Don't forget to try one of the juicy steaks. The dining room even has a themed atmosphere due to an impressive collection of relics and memorabilia from the oil and gas industry. Come find out why The Spudder's claim has been "at steak" for more than forty years.

Monday – Thursday: 5:00 pm to 9:00 pm
Friday & Saturday: 5:00 pm to 10:00 pm

Sea Bass

1 (8-ounce) fillet sea bass
(no more than ¾ inch thick)
Blackening seasoning
2 tablespoons oil

Press bass between paper towels to remove excess water; dry surface with another paper towel. Season entire surface of bass on all sides with blackening seasoning. Add oil to a skillet over high heat; when hot, place fish in skillet. Cook until crispy, then flip and repeat for other side. Stand fillet on edges to crisp. Reduce heat to medium-low and cook until cooked through or bake at 500° for 6 to 8 minutes.

Sauce:

2 tablespoons diced mushrooms
1 tablespoon minced onion
¼ teaspoon minced garlic
1 tablespoon butter
1 tablespoon red wine vinegar
1 teaspoon tomato paste
½ cup heavy cream
Salt and pepper to taste

In a skillet over medium heat, sauté mushrooms, onion and garlic in butter until tender. Add vinegar and reduce until nearly gone. Add tomato paste, cream and salt and pepper; reduce until thickened and sauce coats the back of a spoon. Spoon over sea bass and serve.

Restaurant Recipe

Spudder Potato Soup

4 quarts chicken stock
5 pounds potatoes, diced
1 stick butter
1 cup flour
3 stalks celery, diced
1 large onion, diced
4 cloves garlic, diced
1 quart heavy cream
1 quart milk
1 pound ham, cooked and diced
Salt and pepper to taste

To a stockpot over medium heat, add stock and potatoes; bring to a boil and cook 15 minutes or until fork-tender. Remove potatoes from pot; mash a third of potatoes. In a skillet, melt butter; stir in flour until a roux forms. Add roux to stockpot. In another skillet, sauté celery, onion and garlic until tender; add to stockpot. Add cream, milk and ham along with potatoes. Season with salt and pepper, then simmer 20 to 30 minutes.

Restaurant Recipe

Trenchers Delicatessen

2602 South Harvard Avenue
Tulsa, OK 74114
918-949-3788
Find us on Facebook

Trenchers Delicatessen is a Tulsa favorite that provides distinctive sandwiches to hungry customers. Every sandwich is made using fresh ingredients, all prepared in-house. Trenchers takes pride in roasting and smoking their own deli meats as well as making their own breads, pastries, desserts, condiments, and deli-case selections. In short, they make it all. Diners can create their own sandwiches using the variety of choices offered, so there is something to suit every taste. From sourdough to croissants, roast turkey to chicken salad, and Muenster to Brie, Trenchers can craft your perfect sandwich. The deli even offers vegan options for the meat averse. Visit Trenchers Delicatessen today.

Monday – Saturday: 10:00 am to 3:00 pm

Meatloaf

2 tablespoons unsalted butter
1 onion, chopped
6 ounces white mushrooms, trimmed and thinly sliced
1 tablespoon tomato paste
3 tablespoons plus ½ cup low-sodium chicken stock, divided
2 cloves garlic, minced
2 large eggs
2 tablespoons soy sauce
1 tablespoon unflavored gelatin
½ slice hearty white sandwich bread, torn into 1-inch pieces
⅓ cup minced fresh parsley
2 teaspoons Dijon mustard
¾ teaspoon pepper
½ teaspoon dried thyme
1 pound ground pork
1 pound 85% lean ground beef

Preheat oven to 350°. In a 12-inch skillet over medium heat, melt butter. Add onion and mushrooms; cook 10 to 12 minutes, stirring occasionally. Add tomato paste and cook 3 minutes or until browned. Reduce heat to low; add 3 tablespoons stock and garlic and cook 1 minute until thickened, scraping bottom of skillet to loosen any browned bits. Transfer mixture to a large bowl to cool. In a bowl, whisk together eggs, remaining ½ cup stock and soy sauce; sprinkle gelatin over top and let sit 5 minutes or until softened. In a food processor, pulse bread until finely ground. Add gelatin mixture, mushroom mixture, parsley, mustard, pepper and thyme; pulse until mushrooms are finely ground. Transfer mixture to a large bowl with pork and beef; mix with hands until thoroughly combined. Place a wire rack on a rimmed baking sheet. Fold heavy-duty foil into a 9x5-inch rectangle and place on rack; poke holes in foil ½ inch apart and spray with nonstick spray. Transfer meat mixture to foil and shape into a loaf with hands. Bake on center rack of oven 75 to 90 minutes or until internal temperature reaches 155° to 160°.

Glaze:

½ cup ketchup
¼ cup apple cider vinegar
3 tablespoons packed brown sugar
1 teaspoon hot sauce
½ teaspoon ground coriander seed

In a small saucepan over medium heat, bring all ingredients to a simmer. Cook 5 minutes or until thickened, stirring occasionally. Remove meatloaf from oven and spread half of glaze over meatloaf; return to oven and broil 2 minutes, until glaze bubbles and begins to brown at edges. Remove from oven and spread with remaining glaze; return meatloaf to oven and broil 2 minutes more, until glaze bubbles and begins to brown. Cool meatloaf 20 minutes before slicing and serving.

Restaurant Recipe

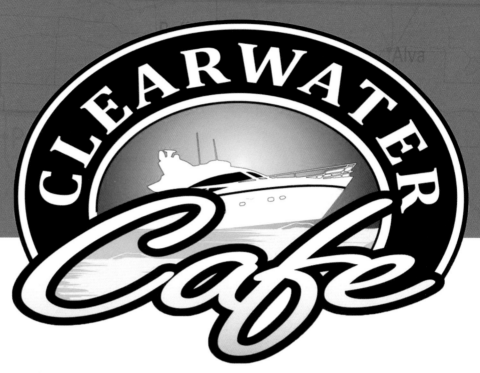

Lake Tenkiller State Park
Vian, OK 74962
918-489-5655
Find us on Facebook

At Pine Cove Marina, you'll discover Clearwater Café. After a day on the lake, a stop at Clearwater Café is just the pick-me-up you will need. Accessible by car or boat, Clearwater Café serves up tasty fare like cheeseburgers, salads, sandwiches, seafood, and steaks. You may dine outside to enjoy your meal with a beautiful backdrop or, if you need to cool off, in the air-conditioned dining area. Whether you choose to visit during the day to enjoy the shaded retreat of the floating patio's colored umbrellas or at night when the twinkling lights sparkle on the lake, you'll always have a good time at Clearwater Café.

Sunday & Thursday: 11:00 am to 7:00 pm
Friday & Saturday: 11:00 am to 9:00 pm

Pork over Rice

3 slices bacon
1 pound lean ground pork
1 medium eggplant, diced
1 cup diced green bell pepper
1 cup diced onion
1 cup diced celery
2 teaspoons ground ginger
½ cup soy sauce
1 (14-ounce) can bean sprouts
½ cup chopped pecans
Steamed rice for serving

In a skillet over medium heat, fry bacon; remove from skillet. Add pork to same skillet; cook, stirring constantly, until cooked through but not browned. Add vegetables and 2 cups water; mix well. Add ginger and soy sauce; cook until vegetables are tender. Add bean sprouts and pecans; cook 5 minutes. Crumble and stir in bacon. Serve over rice.

Local Favorite

Swiss Meatloaf

2 pounds ground beef
1½ cups grated Swiss cheese
2 eggs, beaten
1 onion, grated and sautéed
in butter
½ cup chopped green bell pepper
1½ teaspoons salt
½ teaspoon pepper
1 teaspoon celery salt
2½ cups milk
1 cup breadcrumbs
½ teaspoon paprika

Preheat oven to 350°. In a large bowl, mix all ingredients together until well combined. Press mixture into a greased loaf pan. Bake 1 hour.

Local Favorite

Central

OKLAHOMA

Sid's Diner

300 South Choctaw Avenue
El Reno, OK 73036
405-262-7757
www.sidsdinerelreno.com • Find us on Facebook

Welcome to Sid's Diner, a small-town eatery with good people and good food. Opened in October 1990, Sid's is known for its onion-fried burgers, mouthwatering sandwiches with a

sweet and smoky zest that are made to order right in front of you. The diner also offers delicious coneys smothered in chili and local slaw. Pair your meal with a portion of hand-cut fries served hot and heaping, right out of the basket. Finish your experience with a rich, creamy milkshake, available in a range of flavors, from peanut butter to classic vanilla. Visit Sid's Diner for fantastic food and friendly service.

Monday – Saturday: 7:00 am to 8:00 pm

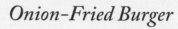

Onion–Fried Burger

These burgers were first served around the time of the Great Depression and have been an Oklahoma staple ever since. Onion burgers at other restaurants are just pale imitations of this Sid's Diner original.

¼ pound ground beef
1 Spanish onion, thinly sliced
Salt and pepper to taste
1 hamburger bun
Pickles to taste
Mustard to taste

Roll beef into a ball and place on a 400°, well-seasoned grill; flatten with spatula. Top with onion and smash with spatula again; season with salt and pepper. Grill 5 minutes on one side, then flip once. Meanwhile, steam and toast bun on grill to absorb onion and beef flavors. To assemble, place burger on bottom bun and finish with pickles and mustard. Top with top bun and enjoy.

Restaurant Recipe

111 North Main Avenue
Goldsby, OK 73093
405-288-2418
www.libbyscafe.com • Find us on Facebook

Libby's Cafe first opened its doors in 1992 under the direction of Scott and Libby Adkins. Libby's is a family-owned and -operated restaurant and full-service bar. The cafe offers a variety of delicious foods, from its famous all-you-can-eat catfish to its certified Black Angus steaks. You don't want to miss out on the chicken-fried steaks covered in homemade gravy. Whether you're looking for a quiet home-style meal to enjoy with family, a place to spend game day with friends, or live music and karaoke, Libby's Cafe has it all. Come dine, drink, and dance. Libby's Cafe awaits your visit.

Tuesday – Thursday: 10:30 am to midnight
Friday: 10:30 am to 2:00 am
Saturday: 8:00 am to 2:00 am
Sunday: 8:30 am to 2:30 pm

Enchilada Casserole

1 pound ground beef
½ cup chopped onion
1 teaspoon garlic powder
½ teaspoon ground cumin
1 (10-ounce) can mild enchilada sauce
1 (12-ounce) package corn tortillas
1 cup shredded Cheddar cheese
1 cup shredded Monterey Jack cheese

Preheat oven to 325°. In a skillet over medium heat, brown beef until crumbly; drain. Add onion, garlic powder, cumin, enchilada sauce. Fill half the enchilada sauce can with water and add to the beef mixture. Simmer 15 minutes, stirring occasionally. Layer tortillas, meat sauce and cheeses in two layers in a greased 9x13-inch baking dish. Bake 15 minutes or until brown and bubbly.

Local Favorite

Baked Apples

4 cooking apples
⅓ cup sugar
¼ teaspoon ground cinnamon
1 tablespoon margarine, cut into quarters

Preheat oven to 350°. Core apples about three-quarters of the way through, leaving a little in the bottom. Place apples in baking pan. Mix sugar and cinnamon; fill centers of apples. Place 1 margarine quarter on top of filling in each apple. Pour ½ cup water in bottom of pan. Bake 45 minutes or until apples are tender. If apples seem dry, spoon liquid in bottom of pan over top of apples during cooking.

Local Favorite

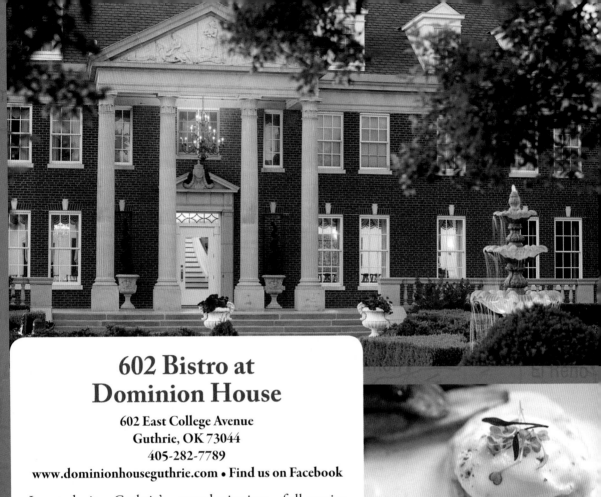

602 Bistro at Dominion House

602 East College Avenue
Guthrie, OK 73044
405-282-7789
www.dominionhouseguthrie.com • Find us on Facebook

Located in Guthrie's award-winning, full-service event venue, Dominion House, 602 Bistro invites you to enjoy delicious fare in an elegant atmosphere. As you step through the door, you'll notice handcrafted woodwork, a grand staircase, and crystal chandeliers. In the dining area, you'll sip on mocktails, signature drinks, and local beer while you indulge in brick-oven pizzas, rice noodles, steaks, seafood, desserts, and more. Finally, be sure to top off your experience with one of the bistro's delicious desserts, from homemade ice creams and crème brûlée to freshly baked cookies. You don't want to miss this unique and delicious experience.

Thursday – Saturday: 5:30 pm to 10:00 pm
Sunday: 11:30 am to 2:30 pm

Blood Orange & Blackberry Sangria

1 (750-milliliter) bottle red wine (pinot noir)

1 (750-milliliter) bottle white wine (chardonnay)

1 cup pineapple juice

1 cup blackberry brandy

1 cup freshly squeezed blood orange juice

1 stick cinnamon

1 cup fresh blueberries

3 blood orange slices

3 to 4 blackberries

In a large pitcher, combine all ingredients, mixing well. Refrigerate at least 24 hours, then serve over ice with a garnish of fresh blueberries, blood orange slices and blackberries.

Restaurant Recipe

STABLES CAFE

223 North Division Street
Guthrie, OK 73044
405-282-0893
http://stablescafe.co • Find us on Facebook

Since 1987, Stables Cafe has operated in the old Tallman Livery Stable building. Owners Marc and Debbie Prather have enjoyed watching Stables go from a small family diner to a thriving restaurant. Serving high-quality meats is Stables' specialty. The menu features country-style classics, like chicken-fried steak, barbecue, steaks, and a customer-favorite salad bar. You can also enjoy Oklahoma craft beer at Taproom223, the in-house bar that opened in 2013. In addition to local beer, the full-service bar also serves frozen margaritas, daiquiris, and more. Combining nostalgic atmosphere with award-winning food and friendly service, Stables Cafe brings you an unforgettable dining experience that will have you coming back for more.

Sunday – Thursday: 11:00 am to 9:00 pm
Friday & Saturday: 11:00 am to 10:00 pm

Mini Onion Rings

2 to 3 yellow onions, thinly sliced
Vanilla milk
Flour for dredging

Preheat deep fryer to 350°. Soak onions in milk for 15 to 20 minutes. Remove onions from milk and toss in flour, pressing them in to coat heavily. Fry for 4 to 5 minutes or until golden brown.

Restaurant Recipe

Chicken-Fried Steak

1 (8-ounce) cube steak,
heavily tenderized
Flour for dredging
Crushed saltine crackers for dredging

Preheat deep fryer to 350°. Moisten both sides of steak with a little water. Dredge steak in flour, pressing to coat each side. Dredge steak in cracker crumbs, pressing to coat each side. Fry until crust is browned and steak is cooked through.

Restaurant Recipe

Lyanna's Lakeside Bar & Grill

10850 South Cedar Road
Hinton, OK 73047
405-284-6788
lyannas-lakeside-bar-grill.business.site • Find us on Facebook

Welcome to Lyanna's Lakeside Bar & Grill, a biker-owned Hinton staple serving up pizza, burgers, beer, and soda. Guests will enjoy a variety of menu options, from tasty starters, like mozzarella sticks, Texas toothpicks, and hot wings, to mouth-watering meals, like half-pound burgers and specialty pizzas. If you're an early riser, the restaurant also serves breakfast specialties, like omelets and Jody's Heart Attack, a hamburger patty on Texas toast topped with fries, fried eggs, white gravy, Cheddar cheese, grilled onions, mushrooms, and bacon pieces. Drop in at Lyanna's for delicious food, thirty-seven different ice-cold beers, live music, and karaoke.

Sunday – Thursday: 11:00 am to 8:00 pm
Friday & Saturday: 11:00 am to 2:00 am

Jody's Heart Attack

1 piece Texas toast, toasted
1 (8-ounce) hamburger patty, cooked
1 potato, sliced and fried
2 eggs, cooked over easy
4 ounces pepper gravy
¼ onion, sliced and grilled
¼ cup crumbled cooked bacon
½ cup sliced mushrooms, grilled

Plate toast and top with hamburger patty. Top with fries and eggs, then cover with gravy. Add onion, bacon and mushrooms.

Restaurant Recipe

Jody's Ultimate Breakfast

1 large biscuit (or 2 pieces Texas toast)
2 sausage patties, cooked
2 eggs, cooked over easy
2 slices bacon, cooked
2 slices Cheddar cheese
1 potato, shredded and fried
4 ounces sausage gravy
Shredded Cheddar cheese for topping

Slice biscuit in half and lay open-faced. Top each biscuit half with a sausage patty, an egg, a slice bacon and a slice cheese. Top each half with half of fried potato. Top both with sausage gravy and shredded Cheddar. Enjoy.

Restaurant Recipe

The Shed

1505 South Main Street
Kingfisher, OK 73750
405-375-4512
Find us on Facebook

At The Shed, there's nothing quite as important as the community. For that reason, the minds behind The Shed have curated a restaurant that feels like a home away from home. Guests will enjoy a menu filled with hand-breaded, scratch-made items as well as comfort food favorites, like Shed burgers, chicken-fried steaks, fried catfish, The Shed Bowl, salads, fried mushrooms, street tacos, nachos, and wraps. If the food doesn't make you feel at home, the cozy space surely will. Kick back on the couches with a drink, a friend, and a game of checkers, or spend some quality time with family in one of the booths. Whether you're making your first or your fiftieth visit, you can be sure The Shed family will make you feel right at home.

Monday – Thursday: 10:30 am to 9:30 pm
Friday & Saturday: 10:30 am to 10:00 pm
Sunday: 10:30 am to 9:00 pm

Taco Salad

Romaine lettuce
Shredded Cheddar cheese to taste
Diced red onion to taste
Diced tomato to taste
Cooked taco meat to taste
Crushed nacho cheese Doritos to taste
1 tablespoon sour cream
Catalina salad dressing to taste

In a shallow bowl, arrange a bed of romaine lettuce. Top with cheese, onion, tomato, taco meat, Doritos and sour cream. Serve with Catalina dressing on the side.

Restaurant Recipe

Red Shed Special

1½ ounces cherry vodka
½ ounce freshly squeezed lime juice
½ ounce freshly squeezed lemon juice
½ ounce simple syrup
½ ounce grenadine
Maraschino cherries for garnish
Lemon wedge for garnish

In a cocktail shaker, combine vodka, lime juice, lemon juice and simple syrup; shake well. Fill a mason jar halfway with ice and strain drink into jar. Top with grenadine and garnish with cherries on a toothpick and a lemon wedge. Enjoy.

Restaurant Recipe

Pelican's Restaurant

291 North Air Depot Boulevard
Midwest City, OK 73110
405-732-4392
www.pelicansok.com • Find us on Facebook

The original Pelican's Restaurant opened in Santa Barbara, California, in the early 1970s, serving seafood and steak dinners. In 1980, after the success of several other locations in California and Texas, Pelican's Restaurant opened its Midwest City location. Today, the restaurant is run by partners Jim Dolezel and Tim Thelin, whose goal is to offer only the finest products and services in a relaxing, casual atmosphere. Guests will enjoy fresh seafood and perfectly aged, hand-cut steaks as well as homemade soups and sauces. Pelican's Restaurant can accommodate parties from 6 to 150, so you'll always have a seat at the table. Or let them bring the food to you with full-service catering. Don't let a good meal pass you by.

Open Daily at 11:00 am

Established 1980

Pasta Primavera

1 ounce garlic butter
1 ounce olive oil
1½ ounces sliced green bell pepper
1½ ounces sliced onion
1½ ounces sliced mushrooms
1½ ounces diced broccoli
1 teaspoon Italian seasoning
4 grape tomatoes, halved
10 ounces fettuccine pasta, cooked
3 ounces shredded Monterey Jack cheese

In a skillet over medium heat, combine garlic butter and olive oil. When hot, add bell pepper, onion, mushrooms, broccoli and Italian seasoning. Cook until onion begins to turn translucent, then add tomatoes; continue cooking until vegetables are tender or to your desired doneness. In an oven-safe dish, plate pasta and top with vegetables and cheese; broil until cheese is melted. Slide pasta onto a new plate and serve. Pairs great with garlic bread or bread sticks.

Restaurant Recipe

Shrimp Cocktail

1 gallon water
1 (12-ounce) can beer of choice
1 tablespoon whole rosemary
2 teaspoons black peppercorns
1 lemon, halved
1 stalk celery, chopped
1 pound frozen jumbo shrimp, thawed

In a large stockpot, combine all ingredients except shrimp; bring to a boil. Carefully add shrimp and cook about 8 minutes or until shrimp are pink and cooked through; remove from heat and drain. Cover shrimp with ice water to prevent further cooking, then let stand until chilled. Serve shrimp as they are or peel first, if desired. Serve in a cocktail glass with lemon wedges and your favorite cocktail sauce or with a side of melted butter.

Restaurant Recipe

The Earth Café & Deli

309 South Flood Avenue
Norman, OK 73069
405-364-3551
www.theearthnorman.com • Find us on Facebook

The Earth Café & Deli's mission is to serve the community and the planet to the best of their ability by offering clean food, minimal waste, and a home away from home where folks can gather to nourish their bodies and souls. Kate and Richard Haas, the café's fourth owners, have been running the café since 2002, but The Earth Café & Deli has been

around since 1969. The café serves breakfast, quiche, soups, nachos, salads, sandwiches, organic smoothies and juices, and so much more. Vegans, vegetarians, and those who are gluten-free are also accommodated. Discover The Earth Café & Deli on your next trip to Norman.

Monday – Friday: 8:00 am to 8:00 pm
Saturday: 9:00 am to 8:00 pm
Sunday: 10:00 am to 5:00 pm

Hummus

2 cups dried garbanzo beans
½ cup extra virgin olive oil
½ cup tahini
½ cup lemon juice
1 head garlic, peeled
Salt to taste
½ bunch fresh parsley
Chips or vegetables for serving

To a saucepan, add beans; cover with water and let soak overnight. Next day, drain beans. Cover with water again and bring to a boil; reduce heat to a simmer and cook 40 to 50 minutes or until tender. Drain beans and add to a food processor with oil, tahini, lemon juice, garlic, salt and parsley; process until creamy, adding water as needed to adjust consistency. Transfer to a serving bowl; serve with chips or vegetables.

Restaurant Recipe

Hollywood Corners

4712 North Porter Avenue
Norman, OK 73071
405-701-4990
Find us on Facebook

Welcome to Hollywood Corners, a 1920s-era gas station and restaurant. The menu features a variety of tasty sandwiches and wraps as well as baked potatoes, baked flatbreads, hot links, barbecue sandwiches, tacos, wings, pizzas, and more. You can also enjoy salads, soups, and sweet treats. The venue regularly hosts live shows featuring local talent and even has an open mic night if you're feeling up to showing off your musical chops. Stop by Hollywood Corners for delicious food and local entertainment.

Sunday – Thursday: 10:30 am to 10:00 pm
Friday & Saturday: 10:30 am to 11:00 pm

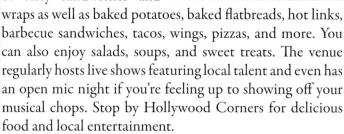

Western Swing Sandwich

1 flatbread
House-made spicy mayonnaise
3 to 4 slices peppered turkey
2 slices Cheddar cheese
3 to 4 slices bacon, cooked crisp
½ avocado, pitted and sliced

Spread flatbread with spicy mayonnaise. Layer turkey and cheese slices, then bacon and avocado. Fold flatbread over, then toast in a toaster oven until cheese is melted and flatbread is crispy. Slice in half and enjoy.

Restaurant Recipe

Franklin Road Melt

1 flatbread
House-made Dijon mayonnaise
3 to 4 slices ham
3 to 4 slices turkey
2 slices Cheddar cheese
2 slices Swiss cheese
1 to 2 slices bacon, cooked crisp
1 to 2 leaves lettuce
1 to 2 slices tomato

Spread flatbread with Dijon mayonnaise. Layer ham, turkey, Cheddar cheese, Swiss cheese, bacon, lettuce and tomato. Fold flatbread over and toast in a toaster oven until cheeses are melted and flatbread is crispy. Slice in half and enjoy.

Restaurant Recipe

LEGEND'S
Restaurant & Catering

1313 West Lindsey Street
Norman, OK 73069
405-329-8888
www.legendsrestaurant.com • Find us on Facebook

Originally opened as a pizza delivery service in 1967, Legend's Restaurant & Catering has seen many changes in its five decades in operation. From pizza, the menu expanded to include salads, steaks, and sandwiches. Over the years, the decor and menu saw many evolutions: dropping the pizza, adding an espresso bar, and even acquiring a banquet facility next door. With time, the restaurant even gleaned accolades from publications like *Bon Appétit* and *Southern Living*. Today, Legend's aspires to serve delicious, healthy, artfully presented food at reasonable prices. Come dine with Legend's Restaurant & Catering today.

Sunday: 10:00 am to 9:00 pm
Monday – Thursday: 11:00 am to 9:00 pm
Friday & Saturday: 11:00 am to 10:00 pm

Legend's Poppy Seed Dressing

⅔ cup white vinegar
¼ cup lemon juice
1½ cups sugar
2 teaspoons dry mustard
2 teaspoons salt
2 cups vegetable oil
3 tablespoons poppy seeds

In a blender, combine vinegar, lemon juice, sugar, mustard and salt; pulse to mix well. With blender running, slowly stream in oil until emulsified. Stir in poppy seeds. Refrigerate before serving.

Restaurant Recipe

Legend's Autumn Nut Torte

5 eggs, separated and divided
1 cup white sugar
2 tablespoons all-purpose flour
¼ teaspoon salt
½ teaspoon baking powder
1 tablespoon orange juice
2 cups grated pecans
¾ cup heavy cream, divided
1½ teaspoons grated orange rind
6 ounces semisweet chocolate chips
2½ cups powdered sugar, divided
1 stick butter
1 cup packed brown sugar

Preheat oven to 350°; grease 2 (8-inch) round cake pans and line with parchment. In a large bowl, beat 4 egg yolks until thickened; whisk in white sugar, flour, salt, baking powder, orange juice and pecans. In another bowl, beat 5 egg whites with an electric mixer until stiff peaks form; fold into pecan mixture. Divide batter between pans, then bake 25 minutes. In a bowl, beat ½ cup cream with an electric mixer until soft peaks form; fold in orange rind. Stack torte layers, frosting between with whipped cream mixture. In a double boiler, melt chocolate, then stir in ½ cup powdered sugar and remaining egg yolk until well blended; frost sides and top of torte. In a saucepan over medium heat, melt butter; whisk in brown sugar, 2 cups remaining powdered sugar and remaining ¼ cup cream; glaze top of torte. Cool and serve.

Restaurant Recipe

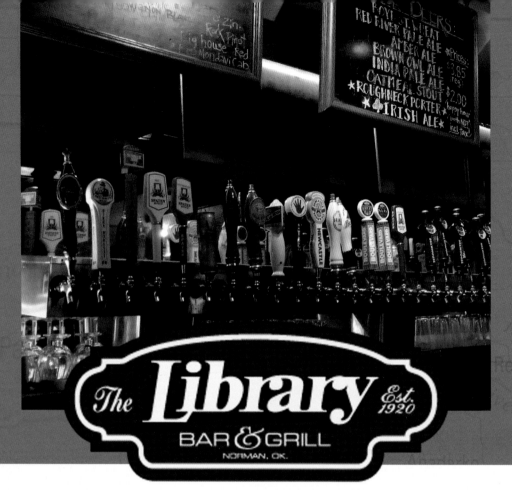

607 West Boyd Street
Norman, OK 73069
405-366-7465
www.gldining.com • Find us on Facebook

Established in the 1920s in a building once used as a home and, later, a dining hall for a fraternity, The Library Bar & Grill is an English-style meetinghouse serving the Norman community. Before it became known as The Library, the eatery was known for many years as Pinks. The stories that locals tell of Pinks make it worth remembering. In 1997, the name was changed to The Library. Ever since, The Library has been providing a friendly neighborhood pub for Norman's fine citizens and visitors. Come on out for brews and delicious grub.

Daily: 11:00 am to 2:00 am

Best Ever Pecan Pie

3 eggs, slightly beaten
1 cup dark corn syrup
1 cup sugar
2 tablespoons butter
1 teaspoon vanilla extract
1½ cups pecans
1 (9-inch) unbaked pie crust

Preheat oven to 350°. In a large bowl, mix all ingredients except pecans until well blended. Stir in pecans; pour mixture into pie crust. Bake 50 to 55 minutes or until knife inserted into center comes out clean. Cool and serve.

Local Favorite

Cheese Marbles

2 cups grated Cheddar cheese
½ cup butter, softened
1 cup flour
¼ teaspoon salt
2 teaspoons dry mustard

Preheat oven to 350°. In a bowl, blend cheese and butter until smooth and creamy. In a bowl, sift together flour, salt and mustard; add to cheese mixture, mixing thoroughly. Form into marble-size balls and place on a greased baking sheet. Bake 15 minutes and enjoy.

Local Favorite

The Mont

1300 Classen Boulevard
Norman, OK 73071
405-329-3330
www.themont.com • Find us on Facebook

A Norman staple for more than forty years, The Mont was opened by a trio of fraternity brothers from the University of Oklahoma on Halloween of 1976. John Krattiger, Bill Hammons, and Dick Talley had watched for many years as restaurant after restaurant opened and closed in the historic building at Boyd Street and Classen Boulevard. When opportunity presented itself, the partners took the chance, and the rest is history. Today, guests can still enjoy the same tasty dishes that made The Mont popular all those years ago, like clubs, burgers, queso, nachos, fried chicken, enchiladas, tacos, and so much more. You'll always enjoy great food when you visit The Mont.

Daily: 11:00 am to 2:00 am

Miguel's Club Sandwich

3 slices sourdough bread, toasted
2 tablespoons mayonnaise, divided
1 slice American cheese
3 slices smoked ham
2 leaves lettuce, divided
4 slices tomato, divided
1 slice Swiss cheese
3 slices smoked turkey
2 slices bacon, cooked crisp

Layer sandwich as follows: Spread 1 slice sourdough with 1 tablespoon mayonnaise. Add American cheese, ham, 1 leaf lettuce and 2 slices tomato. Add another slice sourdough and spread with remaining mayonnaise. Add Swiss cheese, turkey, remaining lettuce, remaining tomato and bacon. Finish with last slice sourdough and pin sandwich along each edge with 4 toothpicks; cut on a diagonal both ways. Serve with fries or chips.

Restaurant Recipe

Buffalo Wings

Mild Sauce:

1 cup melted butter
1 cup Frank's RedHot hot sauce
1 teaspoon white vinegar
1 teaspoon Head Country barbecue sauce

In a bowl, mix all ingredients until combined; set aside.

Hot Sauce:

1 cup melted butter
1 cup Frank's RedHot sauce
1 teaspoon Head Country barbecue sauce
1 tablespoon cayenne pepper

In a bowl, mix all ingredients until combined; set aside.

Wings:

2 cups all-purpose flour
1 teaspoon pepper
1 teaspoon seasoned salt
1 teaspoon garlic powder
2 pounds raw chicken wings, cleaned

Preheat deep fryer to 375°. In a bowl, whisk together flour and seasonings; toss wings in flour mixture and fry 10 to 15 minutes or until internal temperature reaches 165°. Toss wings in prepared mild or hot sauce. Buffalo wings pair perfectly with celery, carrot sticks, and ranch or blue cheese dressing.

Restaurant Recipe

Ozzie's Diner

1700 Lexington Avenue
Norman, OK 73069
405-364-9835
Find us on Facebook

Established in 1987, Ozzie's Diner is located inside the Max Westheimer Airport. The restaurant is home to delicious, classic diner grub. Ozzie's is known for its all-you-can-eat breakfast, which features favorites like pancakes, biscuits, eggs, toast, grits, and hash browns. Be sure to order the fan favorite: the hearty, peppery skillet home fries and onions. For lunch, try the patty melt or the roadhouse fried chicken. If the friendly wait staff and low-priced food weren't enough, diners also enjoy spectacular views of airplanes as they depart from or arrive at the airport. Visit today for some of the best diner food in the metro.

Monday – Saturday: 6:00 am to 9:00 pm
Sunday: 6:00 am to 3:00 pm

Chicken & Dumplings

36 eggs
¼ cup chicken granules
5 pounds all-purpose flour
1 tablespoon baking powder
2 cups ⅛-inch-thick carrot slices
2 cups chopped onion
2 cups chopped celery
4 sticks butter
20 pounds chicken leg quarters

In a large bowl, combine eggs, chicken granules, flour and baking powder; mix well and turn out onto a floured surface. Roll out to ¼-inch thickness; rest 30 minutes. Meanwhile, sauté vegetables in butter until tender; set aside. In a large stockpot, combine chicken legs and 3 to 3½ gallons water; bring to a boil. Cut dumplings to desired size and add to pot; boil 25 to 30 minutes. Stir in sautéed vegetables until heated through and enjoy.

Restaurant Recipe

Cream Pies

6 (9-inch) frozen deep-dish
pie crusts, thawed
3 quarts milk
12 egg yolks
1¼ cups melted butter
1¼ cups cornstarch
2½ cups sugar
3 teaspoons vanilla extract

Preheat oven to 425°. Bake pie crusts 15 minutes, then cool. In a saucepan over medium-low heat, warm milk to a simmer. In a mixing bowl, combine remaining ingredients; add mixture to milk when it begins to simmer and stir vigorously until it thickens. Simmer filling 30 seconds to 1 minute. Divide between pie crusts and refrigerate until completely chilled.

Restaurant Recipe

Scratch Kitchen & Cocktails

132 West Main Street
Norman, OK 73069
405-801-2900
www.eatatscratch.com
Find us on Facebook

At Scratch Kitchen & Cocktails, you'll discover a team that is self-described as "nerds about flavor." Food fills their thoughts between meals. They even spend their free time honing their knife skills, studying spices, dissecting spirits, and doing whatever else is required to better prepare daring, delicious feasts. The team understands that their reputation is forged in the kitchen and behind the bar, so good food is the best advertising. The service may be incredibly friendly, but you can always expect a mean plate. The best part is that everything is prepared from scratch. You'll definitely taste the difference.

Monday – Wednesday: 11:00 am to 11:00 pm
Thursday & Friday: 11:00 am to midnight
Saturday: 9:00 am to midnight
Sunday: 9:00 am to 3:00 pm

Whiskey Smash

1 cup light brown sugar
¾ cup maple syrup
¼ cup bourbon
1½ tablespoons fresh lemon juice
5 to 7 fresh mint leaves
2 (3x½-inch) strips lemon peel
1 mint sprig

In a medium saucepan, bring 2 cups water to a simmer. Remove from heat; gradually whisk in brown sugar until dissolved. Whisk in syrup and cool completely. In a cocktail shaker, add 1½ tablespoons prepared syrup; store remaining syrup in an airtight container in refrigerator. To cocktail shaker, add bourbon, lemon juice, mint leaves, lemon peel and ice to fill. Shake vigorously until thoroughly chilled, then pour through a wire-mesh strainer into a whiskey glass filled with ice. Slap mint sprig to awaken oils, then place in drink. Enjoy.

Restaurant Recipe

Steak au Poivre

2 tablespoons green peppercorns
½ cup white vinegar
1 tablespoon butter
2 tablespoons olive oil, divided
1¼ pounds beef tenderloin trimmings, cut into ½-inch pieces
2 slices hickory-smoked bacon, chopped
2 cups chopped onion
1 cup each chopped celery and carrot
1 tablespoon black peppercorns
3 cloves garlic, crushed
¼ cup tomato paste
1 bay leaf
1 cup each dry white wine and brandy
2 quarts beef stock
4 (12-ounce) beef strip steaks
2 teaspoons kosher salt
3 tablespoons mixed whole peppercorns
1 tablespoon coriander seeds
1 cup heavy cream
1 tablespoon cognac
1 teaspoon lemon juice

In a saucepan, combine green peppercorns, vinegar and ½ cup water; bring to a boil, remove from heat and set aside 1 hour. Strain and reserve peppercorns. Heat butter and 1 tablespoon oil in a Dutch oven over medium-high heat; add trimmings and cook 8 to 12 minutes until browned. Add bacon; cook until it begins to crisp. Add vegetables, black peppercorns and garlic; cook 6 minutes until vegetables are tender and onion starts to brown. Reduce heat to medium-low, then add tomato paste and bay leaf; cook 1 minute until paste thickens. Stir in wine and brandy and increase heat to medium-high; cook 10 minutes until reduced. Add stock and boil 70 minutes until reduced by half. Pour mixture through a cheesecloth-lined strainer; discard solids. Wipe Dutch oven clean; add 2 cups prepared sauce and reserved green peppercorns. Boil 15 minutes until reduced to 1 cup; set aside. Sprinkle steaks on both sides with salt. In a coffee grinder, coarsely process mixed peppercorns and coriander seeds; rub each side of steaks with 1 teaspoon peppercorn mixture. Heat remaining oil in a 12-inch ovenproof skillet over medium-high heat. Cook steaks 2 minutes or until browned. Flip steaks; place skillet in 400° oven, baking 6 minutes or until internal temperature reaches 140°. Transfer to plates and rest 3 minutes. Stir heavy cream and cognac into prepared sauce over low heat. When heated, remove from heat and stir in lemon juice. Serve steaks with sauce.

Restaurant Recipe

Ann's Chicken Fry House

4106 Northwest 39th Street
Oklahoma City, OK 73112
405-943-8915

For decades, Ann's Chicken Fry House has served locals and visitors delicious home-style food. This Route 66 landmark has a cozy atmosphere but limited seating, so it's best to arrive before the rush to ensure you get a seat. True to its name, the restaurant serves up tasty fried chicken with all the sides you could ever need, from homemade mashed potatoes and gravy to fried green tomatoes. You'll also enjoy chicken-fried steaks, salads, chili, hamburgers, and more. Save room for a dessert of deep-fried peaches or coconut pie. Come see for yourself why Ann's Chicken Fry House is an OKC staple.

Tuesday – Saturday: 11:00 am to 8:30 pm

Fried Green Tomatoes

1 quart vegetable oil for frying
1 cup flour
2 teaspoons salt
¼ teaspoon pepper
1 cup buttermilk
4 large green tomatoes, sliced

In a saucepan, heat oil to 350°. In a shallow bowl, whisk together flour, salt and pepper. To another bowl, add buttermilk. One slice at a time, dip tomatoes into flour mixture then into buttermilk. Dredge in flour mixture again, then carefully place in hot oil. Fry tomato slices until browned. Drain on paper towels before serving.

Restaurant Recipe

Green Beans

1 gallon fresh green beans
½ cup chopped onion
1 tablespoon beef base
2 strips bacon

In a large saucepan, combine all ingredients. Set heat to high and bring to boil. Boil 5 minutes. Cool before serving.

Restaurant Recipe

Bedlam BAR-B-Q

610 Northeast 50th Street
Oklahoma City, OK 73105
405-528-RIBS (7427)
www.bedlambarbq.com • Find us on Facebook

Bedlam BAR-B-Q prepares meats in the old traditions of curing and dry-rub applications. The barbecue joint uses family recipes that are held carefully and diligently to the original standards, each passed down to children by their parents. Bedlam BAR-B-Q began serving Oklahoma City in 2003. The Northeast 50th Street location is central to the forgotten homes of many founding community pioneers, such as Tom Braniff, Beverly Osborne, Harvey Everest, Bill Payne, General William S. Key, Mont Highly, R. J. Edwards, General Clyde J. Watts, Byron Gambulos, and even "The Gold Brothers," John and Peter Sinopoulo. Bedlam BAR-B-Q is honored to bring traditional barbecue to Oklahomans and travelers alike.

Monday – Thursday: 10:30 am to 9:00 pm
Friday & Saturday: 10:30 am to 10:00 pm
Sunday: 11:00 am to 3:00 pm

Cowboy Beans

½ cup chopped red onion

2 tablespoons butter

2 (108-ounce) cans ranch-style beans

6 to 8 jalapeños, deseeded
and chopped

⅓ cup chili powder

In a skillet over medium heat, sauté onion in butter until translucent. To a stockpot over medium heat, add beans. Add sautéed onion to beans, then stir in jalapeños and chili powder until incorporated. Cook 30 minutes or until heated through. Makes 2 gallons or about 50 servings.

Restaurant Recipe

Pasta Salad

4 pints macaroni noodles

1 red bell pepper, chopped

1 yellow bell pepper, chopped

1 orange bell pepper, chopped

1 green bell pepper, chopped

4 to 6 stalks celery, chopped

2 cups chopped red onion

½ cup mustard

1½ cups sweet relish

3 cups mayonnaise

1 cup ranch dressing

In a stockpot, boil noodles per package directions; remove from heat. Shock noodles by adding 2 to 3 cups ice to water. When noodles are cold, drain water. Add remaining ingredients and stir until evenly combined. Makes 1 gallon.

Restaurant Recipe

EMPIRE
SLICE HOUSE

1804 Northwest 16th Street
Oklahoma City, OK 73106
405-557-1760
www.empireslicehouse.com
Find us on Facebook

Empire Slice House is a pizza restaurant and bar located in Oklahoma City's beloved Plaza District. The pizza joint serves New York–style pies and pizza by the slice. You'll enjoy inventive specialty pizzas like the Figgy Stardust, a combination of pesto, mozzarella, roasted chicken, ham, and tasty figs. You can also kick it up a notch with the Ghostface Killah, a pie made with ghost pepper marinara, mozzarella, pepperoni, poblanos and crunchy barbecue chips. Empire Slice also boasts a full bar with six rotating taps, delicious wines, cocktails, and a wide selection of canned beers. Visit Empire Slice House, where you can live free and pie hard.

Monday – Saturday: 11:00 am to 1:30 am
Sunday: 11:00 am to midnight

Ghostface Killah Pizza

1 (10- to 12-inch) homemade or store-bought pizza crust
Ghost chile marinara to taste
Shredded mozzarella cheese to taste
Sliced pepperoni to taste
Sliced roasted poblano peppers to taste
Crushed barbecue chips to taste

Preheat oven to 475°. Place pizza crust on a pizza stone. Generously spread with marinara, leaving a 1-inch border around the perimeter. Top with mozzarella. Add pepperoni, poblanos and barbecue chips. Bake 10 to 15 minutes or until crust is browned and cheese is golden. Slice and enjoy.

Restaurant Recipe

Foghorn Leghorn Pizza

1 (10- to 12-inch) homemade or store-bought pizza crust

Sweet marinara sauce to taste

Shredded mozzarella cheese to taste

Chopped roasted chicken to taste

Crumbled crispy bacon to taste

Sliced fresh jalapeños to taste

Sriracha sauce for drizzling

Preheat oven to 475°. Place pizza crust on a pizza stone. Generously spread with marinara sauce, leaving a 1-inch border around the perimeter. Top with mozzarella. Add chicken, bacon and jalapeños, then drizzle with sriracha. Bake 10 to 15 minutes or until crust is browned and cheese is golden. Slice and enjoy.

Restaurant Recipe

Figgy Stardust Pizza

1 (10- to 12-inch) homemade or store-bought pizza crust

Basil-almond pesto to taste

Sliced fresh mozzarella to taste

Chopped roasted chicken to taste

Thinly sliced baked ham to taste

Sliced dried Mission figs

Preheat oven to 475°. Place pizza crust on a pizza stone. Generously spread with pesto, leaving a 1-inch border around the perimeter. Top with mozzarella slices, chicken, ham and figs. Bake 10 to 15 minutes or until crust is browned and cheese is golden. Slice and enjoy.

Restaurant Recipe

Mama Roja
Mexican Kitchen

9219 Lake Hefner Parkway
Oklahoma City, OK 73120
405-302-6262
www.mamaroja.com • Find us on Facebook

Dazzle your taste buds at Mama Roja Mexican Kitchen, a restaurant serving up the best border-style Mexican cuisine this side of the Rio Grande. House favorites include street tacos, hand-rolled tamales, sizzling fajitas, and signature plates, like the Pescado Vera Cruz and Fire-Roasted Chicken Chimichanga. Don't forget the chips and queso! The festive, resort-style atmosphere is complimented by a full bar featuring a large variety of tequilas. Grab a pitcher of homemade sangria or perfect margaritas and relax at the lakeside cabana. It's the perfect spot to kick back and watch a gorgeous Oklahoma sunset on Lake Hefner. Mama Roja invites you to join the festivities and dress to chill.

Monday – Wednesday: 11:00 am to 9:00 pm
Thursday – Saturday: 11:00 am to 10:00 pm
Sunday: 10:30 am to 9:00 pm

Roja Shaker

Anaheim chiles
El Jimador Blanco tequila
Cointreau
House-made margarita mix
Ice
Sliced lime for garnish
Arbol chile for garnish

Marinate Anaheim chiles in tequila at least 4 days; strain out chiles and reserve tequila. In a tin shaker, combine chile-infused tequila, Cointreau, margarita mix and ice; shake well. Serve in a salt-rimmed martini glass with a lime slice and an Arbol chile.

Restaurant Recipe

Fajitas

House-marinated chicken, steak or shrimp
Sliced bell peppers and onions
House-made fajita juice
House-made fajita seasoning
Guacamole, pico de gallo, sour cream and mixed cheeses for serving
Warm freshly made flour tortillas for serving
Beans or Mexican rice for serving

Grill chicken, steak or shrimp to order. In a skillet over medium-high heat, sauté bell peppers and onions in house-made fajita juice and house-made fajita seasoning until tender; transfer to a sizzling skillet and top with chicken, steak or shrimp. Serve with guacamole, pico de gallo, sour cream, mixed cheeses, tortillas, and beans or rice on the side.

Restaurant Recipe

The Press

1610 North Gatewood Avenue
Oklahoma City, OK 73106
405-208-7739
www.thepressokc.com • Find us on Facebook

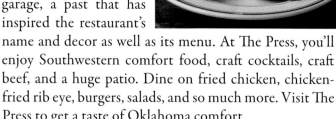

Located in a 1948-dated building in Oklahoma City's Plaza district, The Press serves breakfast, lunch, and dinner like you've never had before. The building was once home to a printing press and garage, a past that has inspired the restaurant's name and decor as well as its menu. At The Press, you'll enjoy Southwestern comfort food, craft cocktails, craft beef, and a huge patio. Dine on fried chicken, chicken-fried rib eye, burgers, salads, and so much more. Visit The Press to get a taste of Oklahoma comfort.

Tuesday – Friday: 11:00 am to 10:00 pm
Saturday & Sunday: 10:00 am to 10:00 pm

Ham, Cheese & Rice

1 onion, sliced
1 tablespoon oil
¾ cup rice
1½ cups cubed cooked ham
¼ teaspoon salt
½ cup milk
⅔ cup cubed cheese

In a saucepan over medium heat, cook onion in oil until lightly browned. Add 1¾ cups water and heat to boiling. Stir in rice, ham and salt. Cover, reduce heat to low and cook 25 minutes or until rice is tender. Gently stir in milk and cheese. Heat until cheese is melted.

Local Favorite

Slow Cooker Barbecued Chicken

1 (4-pound) fryer, cut up
1 (10-ounce) bottle ketchup
1 onion, chopped
10 ounces Coca-Cola
Salt and pepper to taste

Place chicken, ketchup, onion, Coca-Cola and salt and pepper in a slow cooker. Cook on low overnight. Remove bones from chicken. Best served over hot rice.

Local Favorite

The Range Café

615 West Wilshire Boulevard, Suite 1400
Oklahoma City, OK 73116
405-608-4999
www.wilshiregun.com • Find us on Facebook

Located inside the Wilshire Gun shooting range, The Range Café serves up a variety of tasty dishes. Choose from primers like chips and queso, hand-breaded fried pickles, boneless wings, and more. Settle down to entrées like steak, pot roast, bison chili, shrimp baskets, and chicken tenders. You can also order from a selection of handhelds that includes burgers, Reuben sandwiches, chicken sandwiches, BLTs, pulled pork sandwiches, and chicken-fried steak sandwiches. Pair your meal with one of The Range Café's on-tap draft beers, import beers, domestic beers, or wines. Don't leave without dessert, such as an apple turnover, bread pudding, or vanilla ice cream. You'll find something to hit the spot.

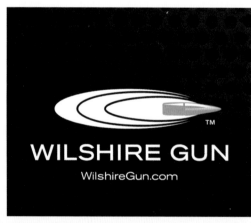

Tuesday – Saturday: 11:00 am to 8:00 pm
Sunday: 11:00 am to 6:00 pm

Hobo Stew

1 cup thinly sliced onion

1 cup chopped green bell pepper

¼ cup vegetable oil

1 pound ground beef

1 (15-ounce) can pinto beans, drained

1 (15-ounce) can whole-kernel corn, drained

1 (32-ounce) can Italian-style tomatoes

2 (8-ounce) cans tomato sauce

1 tablespoon steak sauce

Dried basil, dry mustard, salt and pepper to taste

In a large skillet over medium heat, cook onion and bell pepper in oil until golden brown. Add beef, cooking until just browned. Add remaining ingredients and mix well. Cover and simmer 15 to 20 minutes.

Local Favorite

Easy Chocolate Pie

1 (9-inch) unbaked pie crust

1 cup plus 3 tablespoons sugar, divided

2 tablespoons cocoa powder

3 tablespoons flour

2 eggs, separated

2 cups milk

1 tablespoon butter

1 teaspoon vanilla extract

Preheat oven to 400°. Using a fork, poke holes in bottom and sides of pie crust; bake 9 to 12 minutes. Remove from oven and set aside. In a saucepan, mix together 1 cup sugar, cocoa and flour. Add egg yolks and milk, stirring well. Add butter and vanilla and place over medium heat until mixture thickens; pour into pie crust. Beat egg whites until stiff. Add remaining 3 tablespoons sugar and beat until fluffy. Top pie with meringue; bake until top is golden brown.

Local Favorite

Sean Cummings' Irish Restaurant

7628 North May Avenue
Oklahoma City, OK 73116
405-841-7326
www.seancummings-ok.com
Find us on Facebook

Sean Cummings grew up with a father from Galway, a city in the province of Connacht, in Ireland. Sean grew up eating dishes like colcannon, a mash of potatoes, cabbage, leeks, and bacon. This is the kind of Irish cuisine you can expect at Sean Cummings'. Inside the softly lit pub, you'll discover traditional Irish music and a smattering of Irish memorabilia that adorns the walls. With inspired food, Guinness on draught, and music that binds the patrons, it's easy to see why the restaurant has become an OKC staple. Visit Sean Cummings' Irish Restaurant to discover the time-honored traditions of hospitality, great food, great music, and the perfect pint. *Sláinte*!

Monday – Thursday: 4:00 pm to midnight
Friday & Saturday: 4:00 pm to 2:00 am
Sunday: 4:00 pm to 10:00 pm

Colcannon

1 pound bacon, chopped and cooked

3 pounds potatoes, chopped
and boiled

2 cups boiled cabbage

2 leeks, cleaned, chopped and
boiled 4 minutes

½ cup chopped fresh parsley

1 cup whole milk

2 teaspoons butter

Salt and pepper to taste

In a large bowl, combine all ingredients. Mash and mix until well combined. Serve Colcannon with Irish Brown Bread.

Family Favorite

Potato Soup

3 slices raw bacon, chopped
1 quart chicken stock
5 potatoes, peeled and chopped
½ cup chopped green onion
1 pint heavy cream
½ teaspoon freshly ground pepper

In a large metal stockpot, cook bacon over low heat, taking care not to burn; do not drain bacon fat. Add stock and potatoes; bring to a boil and cook until potatoes are tender. Add remaining ingredients, bring back to a boil and cook until heated through. If you would like a thicker soup, crush potatoes against the side of the pot and stir until thickened. Serve with Irish Brown Bread.

Family Favorite

Irish Brown Bread

4 cups all-purpose flour
4 cups stone-ground whole-wheat flour,
plus 1 tablespoon for dusting
½ cup steel-cut oats
2 tablespoons baking powder
2 tablespoons baking soda
½ teaspoon salt
½ teaspoon packed brown sugar
¼ pound cold butter
1 quart buttermilk

Preheat oven to 425°. In a large bowl, combine both all-purpose flour, whole-wheat flour, oats, baking powder, baking soda, salt and brown sugar. Using a grater, grate butter into dry ingredients; toss together. Add buttermilk and mix loosely. Gather dough into a large loaf and place on a greased baking sheet. Score top of dough with a knife in the shape of a pound sign (#). Dust top of bread with remaining 1 tablespoon flour and bake 40 minutes. Bread is done when internal temperature reaches 180°.

Family Favorite

Paul's Place Steakhouse

120 West MacArthur Street, Suite 104
Shawnee, OK 74804
405-275-5650
www.paulsplacesteakhouse.com
Find us on Facebook

Paul's Place Steakhouse is a locally owned and operated grill and full-service bar that serves up steak, seafood, and so much more. Sample all-day specials, from appetizers and entrées to plate lunches and refreshing salads. Though Paul's Place specializes in hand-cut steaks, you can also enjoy featured lunch specials, like homemade meatloaf, chicken-fried chicken, chicken-fried steak, and hand-breaded catfish. The restaurant even serves eleven lunch specials under $7.99 and is Blue Zone–certified. The range of menu options is virtually endless and ever-changing. Whether you dine in, order takeout, or reserve catering, you'll always find something new and interesting to satisfy your palate.

Lunch:
Tuesday – Friday: 11:00 am to 2:00 pm
Dinner:
Tuesday – Thursday: 4:30 pm to 8:30 pm
Friday & Saturday: 4:30 pm to 9:00 pm

Brownies

16 ounces bittersweet chocolate, chopped and divided

1 stick butter

6 eggs

2 cups sugar

2 teaspoons vanilla extract

½ cup all-purpose flour

¼ cup cocoa powder

2 teaspoons baking powder

1 teaspoon salt

½ cup sour cream

1 cup chopped walnuts

Bring 2 to 3 cups water to a simmer in a double boiler; place 10 ounces chocolate and butter in the top pot, then stir until melted. Add eggs, sugar and vanilla to a bowl and whisk until light yellow. When chocolate is melted, whisk slowly into egg mixture. In another bowl, sift together dry ingredients; fold into wet mixture until smooth. Whisk is sour cream until smooth. Pour batter into a buttered 9x13-inch dish, spreading evenly. Sprinkle with walnuts and remaining 6 ounces chocolate. Bake at 300° for 50 minutes or until firm but moist in the center; cool before cutting.

Restaurant Recipe
Chef Neil Lindenbaum

Chicken & Grilled Corn Chowder

⅛ cup olive oil

6 (3-inch) ears corn, grilled and kernels cut from cobs

1 green Anaheim chile, seeded and diced

½ red onion, chopped

⅔ cup chopped celery

⅔ cup diced carrot

⅔ cup diced red bell pepper

1 jalapeño, seeded and diced

1 pound cooked chicken, diced

1 gallon chicken broth

1 pint heavy cream

1 tablespoon minced fresh thyme

1 clove garlic, chopped

1 bay leaf

Pinch cayenne pepper

Salt and pepper to taste

2 cups cornstarch

In a large stockpot over medium heat, combine olive oil and chopped vegetables; sauté 5 minutes, then stir in chicken. Add ¼ cup water and remaining ingredients except cornstarch. Slowly stir in cornstarch until dissolved. Set heat to low and simmer gently 30 minutes.

Restaurant Recipe
Chef Neil Lindenbaum

WHERE IT'S GOOD TO BE BAD

BAD BRAD'S
· BAR-B-Q ·
JOINT

Stillwater location:
3317 East 6th Avenue
Stillwater, OK 74074
405-377-4141

Yukon location:
700 West Main Street
Yukon, OK 73099
405-354-2122

www.badbrads.com • Find us on Facebook

Bad Brad's Bar-B-Q is a locally owned and operated barbecue joint serving Oklahoma- and Texas-style barbecue smoked the old-fashioned way. Keeping with the old, tried-and-true ways means Bad Brad's uses no electricity or gas to craft its delicious barbecue. All the magic happens in wood-fired pits, which add an unbeatable heavy smoke flavor to all of the restaurant's meats. Bad Brad's also buys local whenever and wherever possible and uses dry rubs and regional woods to bring out the best flavor every time. Come enjoy tasty barbecue in the down-home, laid-back, rustic atmosphere at Bad Brad's, where it's good to be bad.

Monday – Thursday: 11:00 am to 8:30 pm
Friday & Saturday: 11:00 am to 9:00 pm

Lasagna Casserole

1 pound ground beef
¼ cup chopped onion
½ teaspoon salt
½ teaspoon pepper, divided
1 pound medium pasta shells, cooked and drained
4 cups shredded part-skim mozzarella cheese, divided
3 cups 4% cottage cheese
2 large eggs, lightly beaten
⅓ cup grated Parmesan cheese
2 tablespoons dried parsley
1 (24-ounce) jar pasta sauce

In a large skillet, cook beef and onion over medium heat until meat is no longer pink; drain. Sprinkle with salt and ¼ teaspoon pepper; set aside. In a large bowl, combine pasta, 3 cups mozzarella cheese, cottage cheese, eggs, Parmesan cheese, parsley and ¼ teaspoon remaining pepper. Transfer to a greased shallow 3-quart baking dish. Top with beef mixture and pasta sauce (dish will be full). Cover and bake at 350° for 45 minutes. Sprinkle with remaining 1 cup mozzarella cheese. Bake, uncovered, 15 minutes longer or until bubbly and cheese is melted. Let stand for 10 minutes before serving.

Local Favorite

Baked Ham

1 (10- to 15-pound) fully cooked ham
2 cups white sugar
1 cup apple cider vinegar
1 stick cinnamon
12 whole cloves plus extra cloves to stud ham
6 allspice berries
Pepper if desired
1 (15-ounce) can sliced pineapple plus juice
1½ cups brown sugar

Preheat oven to 350°. Wash ham and place in large roasting pan with lid. Add white sugar, vinegar, cinnamon stick, cloves and allspice berries. Cook 15 minutes per pound, turning ham often. Remove from oven and cool. Lower oven to 250°. Remove top skin, leaving fat on ham. Place ham in clean roasting pan and stud with extra cloves and pineapple slices. Spread brown sugar over ham. Pour pineapple juice in pan. Bake 1 hour. After 30 minutes, baste every 10 minutes. Remove from oven; keep covered and warm until ready to serve.

Local Favorite

FREDDIE PAUL'S STEAKHOUSE

1707 East 6th Avenue
Stillwater, OK 74074
405-377-8777
www.freddiepauls.com • Find us on Facebook

Brian Saliba grew up watching his grandparents and parents run their own restaurants. From a young age, he displayed a love for the business and decided to pursue a career in

the culinary arts. He studied hotel and restaurant administration at Oklahoma State University, interned at The Broadmoor in Colorado Springs, apprenticed at The Greenbrier hotel and resort in West Virginia, and worked at The Mansion in Dallas. With a lifetime of training under his belt, Brian and his wife, Joie, opened Freddie Paul's Steakhouse, the next in generations of Saliba family restaurants and Brian and Joie's dream come true. Drop by for delicious steaks, sandwiches, and so much more.

Monday – Friday: 11:00 am to 10:00 pm
Saturday & Sunday: 11:00 am to 10:00 pm

Cabbage Rolls

1 head cabbage
Ground beef, uncooked
Tomato sauce
Rice, uncooked
Garlic powder
Freddie Paul's grill seasoning
Ground cinnamon

In a large stockpot, cover cabbage with water; bring to a boil and cook until outer leaves easily pull away. Meanwhile, in a separate bowl, combine beef, tomato sauce, rice, garlic powder, seasoning and cinnamon, adjusting quantities as desired. Mix in a few tablespoons water to add moisture to mixture. Peel off cabbage leaves and cut out thick veins at the bottom of each; add meat mixture to each leaf, overlap cut ends and roll up, tucking in sides as you go. Repeat for each roll. Slice remaining cabbage and line the bottom of a lidded, ovenproof Dutch oven; place cabbage rolls seam-side down on top of sliced cabbage. Top rolls with additional tomato sauce. Cover and bake at 350° for 1½ hours or until rolls are tender. Enjoy.

Restaurant Recipe

Tabouli

Minced onion
Cracked wheat, prepared per package directions
Diced tomato
Extra virgin olive oil
Lemon juice
Freddie Paul's grill seasoning
Chopped fresh parsley

In a large bowl, toss together all ingredients until evenly incorporated, adjusting quantities to taste. Cover with plastic wrap and refrigerate at least 30 minutes. Transfer to a serving platter or to individual plates. Tabouli pairs perfectly with a side of toasted pita and romaine lettuce leaves.

Restaurant Recipe

701 South Main Street
Stillwater, OK 74074
405-743-1299
www.grannyskitchenstillwater.com • Find us on Facebook

When you dine at Granny's Kitchen, you aren't just eating at one of the best breakfast joints in Oklahoma. You are biting into some rich history. Though the name has changed over the years, the restaurant's location, family, and flavors date back to 1945, when the restaurant was called Niles Café. It was later purchased by the Rains family and went through several name changes and face-lifts before finally becoming Granny's Kitchen in 1983. Come settle in at Granny's Kitchen, where you'll enjoy down-home dishes as well as the feeling of being home with family and being a part of the Stillwater community.

Monday – Friday: 6:00 am to 2:00 pm
Saturday & Sunday: 6:00 am to 3:00 pm

Granny's Own Meatloaf

½ cup minced onion

½ cup minced green bell pepper

2 tablespoons butter

Salt to taste

½ cup breadcrumbs (or panko)

1 tablespoon granulated garlic

1 tablespoon Lawry's seasoned salt
(or your favorite seasoning blend)

½ cup milk

2 pounds ground beef

¼ cup ketchup (or tomato paste) plus
more for glazing

1 tablespoon A.1. steak sauce
(or barbecue sauce)

Preheat oven to 325°. In a skillet, sauté onion and bell pepper in butter. Season with salt and cool to room temperature. In a bowl, mix breadcrumbs, garlic, Lawry's and milk to form a paste. In another bowl, mix beef with sautéed veggies. Mix breadcrumb paste and ketchup with beef until incorporated. Transfer to a greased loaf pan, cover with foil and bake 35 minutes. Rotate pan and bake 25 minutes more. Remove foil and rest 5 to 15 minutes; free edges and flip meatloaf onto a baking sheet. Glaze with ketchup and steak sauce; bake 10 to 20 minutes to set sauce. Enjoy.

Restaurant Recipe

How to Fry Anything Granny's Way

6 large eggs

1 cup buttermilk

2 tablespoons finely ground pepper

1 tablespoon Lawry's seasoned salt

1 tablespoon coarsely ground pepper

1 tablespoon sea salt (or kosher salt)

1 tablespoon paprika

2 teaspoons white pepper

2 teaspoons ground thyme

2 cups breadcrumbs (or panko)

2 cups all-purpose flour

Chicken fillets, cube steak or other choice
ingredient to fry

Preheat deep fryer or frying oil to 350°. In a bowl, beat eggs until smooth. Mix in buttermilk, then stir in finely ground pepper and Lawry's. In another bowl, mix coarsely ground pepper, sea salt, paprika, white pepper and thyme; whisk in breadcrumbs, then whisk in flour. Dip chicken fillets, cube steak or other choice ingredient into egg mixture. Remove from egg mixture and dredge in flour mixture. Carefully add dredged ingredient to hot oil and fry until golden brown. Remove from oil and drain on paper towels. In no time, you've got yourself a country-fried dinner.

Family Favorite

The Hideaway

230 South Knoblock Street
Stillwater, OK 74074
405-372-4777
www.theoriginalhideaway.squarespace.com • Find us on Facebook

The Hideaway first opened with three essentials in mind: happy employees, a fun atmosphere, and out-of-this-world pizza. The philosophy remains the same today. A warm, family-friendly atmosphere greets you when you walk through the door. Guests dine on tasty sandwiches, soups, and, of course, pizzas while enjoying attentive service from the staff. Coffee fanatics might like to try handcrafted coffee and espresso drinks from The Daily Grind coffee shop, located inside The Hideaway. Owners Richard and Marti initially bought The Hideaway to help pay for college. Today, they continue that tradition by employing Oklahoma State University students who are working their way through school. Stop by for delicious pizza and help support hardworking students.

Sunday – Thursday: 11:00 am to 10:00 pm
Friday & Saturday: 11:00 am to 11:00 pm

Jordan's Taco Soup

2 tablespoons olive oil
1 cup chopped yellow onion
2 tablespoons ground cumin
1 tablespoon red pepper flakes
1 (1-ounce) packet taco seasoning
1 (1-ounce) packet ranch dressing mix
2 pounds ground beef, browned
and drained
1 (16-ounce) can mild chili
beans, drained
1 (15.25-ounce) can whole-kernel
corn, drained
1 (15-ounce) can pinto beans
1 (14.5-ounce) can diced tomatoes
1 (10-ounce) can Rotel tomatoes
1 (4-ounce) can chopped
green chiles, optional
Salt and pepper to taste

In a large stockpot over medium heat, combine olive oil and onion; sauté onion until translucent. Add spices, taco seasoning and ranch dressing mix. Stir in beef, then add remaining ingredients. Simmer 30 to 45 minutes to blend flavors. Season with salt and pepper. Serve with tortilla chips, shredded Cheddar and your favorite taco toppings.

Restaurant Recipe

Parmesan–Basil Bruschetta

1 tablespoon minced garlic
2 tablespoons olive oil
2 tablespoons balsamic vinegar
¼ cup chopped fresh basil
1 teaspoon salt
1 teaspoon pepper
2 tablespoons grated Parmesan cheese
2 green onions, chopped
4 Roma tomatoes, diced
Shaved Parmesan cheese for garnish

In a bowl, mix together all ingredients except tomatoes and shaved Parmesan. Stir in tomatoes. Enjoy immediately or refrigerate, covered, 24 hours for best flavor. Serve on toasted baguette slices and top with shaved Parmesan.

Restaurant Recipe

The Rock Café

114 West Main Street
Stroud, OK 74079
918-968-3990
www.rockcafert66.com
Find us on Facebook

The Rock Café is an eighty-year-old café located on Route 66. Dawn Welch has owned and operated the restaurant for more than thirty years. In 2001, she was visited by a team from Pixar Animation Studios who were researching Route 66 for the 2006 movie *Cars*. One of the movie's main characters, Sally Carrera, is heavily based on Dawn herself. The inside of the café is adorned with memorabilia from the movie, including signed posters with special dedications from Pixar executives. Dawn and her friends at The Rock Café invite you for an afternoon of fun, delicious food, and history. Just remember to slow down and enjoy!

Daily: 7:00 am to 9:00 pm

Rock Café's Famous Spätzle

4 cups plus ½ cup all-purpose flour, divided
3 large eggs
1 cup milk
Salt to taste

To a large bowl, add 4 cups flour and make a well in the center. In another bowl, whisk together eggs and milk; pour into well and mix with a wooden spoon until dough forms. Add remaining ½ cup flour to a cutting board. With a pizza cutter, cut off a piece of dough and flatten it on cutting board. Cut into strips, then into small pieces and add to a colander. Repeat until all dough is used. Fill a large stockpot three-quarters full with water and add salt to taste; bring to a boil, then add cut dough. Boil 15 minutes, stirring constantly. Drain and rinse, then serve immediately or spread out on baking sheets to dry and freeze. Use as dumplings or substitute as pasta in mac and cheese.

Restaurant Recipe

Peach Cobbler

1 cup all-purpose flour
1½ cups sugar
1 stick butter, melted
2 (16-ounce) cans peaches, drained
Vanilla ice cream for serving, optional

Preheat oven to 375°. In a bowl, whisk together flour and sugar. Drizzle in the melted butter and, using a fork, toss mixture until there are no bits larger than the size of a pea. To a 9-inch, deep-dish pie plate, add peaches. Sprinkle flour mixture over top, then bake 30 to 40 minutes or until golden brown. Cool 10 minutes, then serve with vanilla ice cream, if desired.

Restaurant Recipe

Jäger Sauce

6 strips bacon, chopped
½ cup diced onion
1 cup fresh mushrooms, sliced
1 (0.87-ounce) packet brown gravy mix
2 cups milk
¼ cup paprika

In a skillet over medium heat, sauté bacon, onion and mushrooms until onion is translucent. In a saucepan over medium heat, combine gravy mix and milk and cook until it begins to thicken. Add sautéed mixture and paprika, stirring to mix well. Serve over chicken-fried steak or spätzle.

Restaurant Recipe

The Butcher BBQ Stand

3402 West Highway 66
Wellston, OK 74881
405-240-3437
www.butcherbbqstand.com • Find us on Facebook

After a thirty year stint in the meat business and eight years of competing in the barbecue circuit, the minds behind The Butcher BBQ Stand are serving up their world-championship barbecue to you. Their barbecue has landed them more than seventy grand championships and reserve grand championships, more than four hundred first-place calls, the 2012 World Food Championship, and eight years of nationally ranked barbecue notoriety. Now you can enjoy their delicious barbecue at The Butcher BBQ Stand, Oklahoma's barbecue destination. Dig into some good old-fashioned 'cue while enjoying great music, giant Jenga, and horseshoes. Don't miss out on the chance to try some real, world-famous barbecue.

Open Friday, Saturday & Sunday
Call for Hours

Tea Cakes

1 cup sugar
2 eggs, beaten
¾ cup butter, softened
2 tablespoons milk
3 cups flour

Preheat oven to 350°. In a bowl, mix sugar, eggs, butter and milk. Gradually add flour until well blended. Drop by tablespoonfuls on greased baking sheet. Bake until brown.

Local Favorite

Impossible Taco Pie

The pie does the impossible by making its own crust.

1 pound ground chuck
½ cup chopped onion
1 (1.75-ounce) packet taco
seasoning mix
1 (4-ounce) can green chiles, drained
1¼ cups milk
¾ cup Bisquick Original Pancake
and Baking Mix
3 eggs, beaten
2 tomatoes, sliced
1 cup shredded Monterey Jack or
Cheddar cheese

Preheat oven to 400°. Grease pie plate. To a skillet, cook and stir ground chuck and onion, stirring frequently, until lightly browned; drain. Stir in taco seasoning mix. Spread in pie plate; top with chiles. Beat milk, Bisquick and eggs until smooth. Pour over meat. Bake 25 minutes. Top with tomatoes and cheese; bake another 10 minutes. Cool. May serve with sour cream, chopped tomatoes, shredded lettuce and shredded cheese.

Local Favorite

215 West Chicago Avenue
Yale, OK 74085
918-387-4200
www.mugsysgrubhouse.com
Find us on Facebook

Get ready to eat like a cowboy when you visit Mugsy's Grubhouse. When they opened the restaurant in July 2017, owners Darrell and Jennifer Mueggenborg had one goal in mind for Mugsy's: to provide their customers a meal worthy of their time and expense in a warm, welcoming atmosphere. At Mugsy's, farm-to-table meals are priority, so strict attention is paid to the quality of ingredients used. Enjoy classic comfort food and delicious smoked barbecue. From fried green tomatoes to hand-breaded catfish and calf fries to double-breaded chicken-fried steak, Mugsy's Grubhouse has just what you need to enjoy a meal in true cowboy fashion.

Wednesday – Saturday: 11:00 am to 8:00 pm
Sunday: 11:00 am to 2:00 pm

Chocolate Torte

1½ sticks butter, softened

1½ cups flour

½ cup chopped pecans, optional

Preheat oven to 350°. In a bowl, mix all ingredients until well combined. Press dough into a 9x13-inch baking dish. Bake 15 minutes; cool completely.

Filling:

2 (8-ounce) packages cream cheese, softened

1½ cups powdered sugar

2 teaspoons vanilla extract

1½ cups Cool Whip plus more for topping

2 (3.9-ounce) boxes instant chocolate pudding mix

3 cups cold whole milk

Chocolate curls for garnish

Add cream cheese to a mixing bowl. Using a handheld electric mixer, beat powdered sugar into cream cheese ½ cup at a time until fully incorporated. Beat in vanilla. With a rubber spatula, fold in Cool Whip until combined. Spread onto cooled crust, cover and refrigerate. Meanwhile, add pudding mix and milk to a large bowl; whisk until smooth and creamy. Remove torte from refrigerator and top with pudding mixture, spreading evenly. Finish with a generous layer of Cool Whip and a garnish of chocolate curls.

Family Favorite

Corn Casserole

1 (15-ounce) can whole-kernel corn

1 (14.75-ounce) can cream-style corn

1 (8-ounce) package corn muffin mix

1 stick butter, melted

1 cup sour cream

Salt and pepper to taste

Diced jalapeños (or 1 teaspoon Cajun seasoning), optional

1 to 1½ cups shredded Cheddar-Jack cheese, divided

In a large bowl, mix together whole-kernel corn, cream-style corn, corn muffin mix, butter, sour cream, salt and pepper, jalapeños and ½ cup cheese. Transfer to a well-greased 9x13-inch baking dish. Bake 45 minutes or until golden brown and beginning to set. Remove from oven and top with remaining cheese. Bake 5 to 10 minutes more or until cheese is melted. Let stand several minutes before serving.

Family Favorite

Southeastern

GUEST CHECK

DATE				
SERVER	TABLE		GUESTS	CHECK NUMBER
				689561

1 Cheese burger   5.49
2 Onion Ring   6.88
1 Chicken Wrap   5.99
                 _____
                 16.36

Thank You - Please Come Again

                 17.51
                    .15

189

Pigskins BBQ

1711 Stone Briar Drive
Ada, OK 74820
580-332-3898
Find us on Facebook

Pitmaster Kevin Truett began his journey into the smoky world of barbecue mastery in southern Oklahoma. Shadowing his Uncle Phil, a pitmaster in his own right, Kevin learned the ins and outs of barbecue as a boy. In 2007, Kevin and his wife, Tracy, opened Pigskins BBQ. A daughter and granddaughter of high school football coaches, Tracy thought it only fitting to name the restaurant after a favorite family pastime. The restaurant has enjoyed such success that, twice now, it has required a larger space. Pigskins BBQ has moved to a larger building to meet customer demand, and though the location has changed, the tradition of serving up southern Oklahoma's finest barbecue hasn't.

Monday – Thursday: 11:00 am to 8:00 pm
Friday & Saturday: 11:00 am to 9:00 pm
Sunday: 11:00 am to 3:00 pm

Fried Catfish Breading

12 cups yellow cornmeal
½ cup garlic powder
4 teaspoons salt
2 teaspoons pepper
½ cup Italian seasoning

In a large bowl, whisk together cornmeal, garlic powder, salt, pepper and Italian seasoning. Use for breading catfish fillets before frying.

Restaurant Recipe

Butter Sauce

4 tablespoons butter
½ lemon, zested and juiced
4 cloves garlic, minced
1 tablespoon Dijon mustard
2 tablespoons chopped fresh parsley
1 tablespoon chopped fresh chives
2 teaspoons minced fresh thyme
1 pinch cayenne pepper
¼ teaspoon paprika
¼ teaspoon red pepper flakes
Salt and pepper to taste

In a saucepan over medium heat, melt butter. Add lemon zest and juice and garlic; cook until fragrant, about 1 minute. Stir in mustard, herbs and seasonings until combined. Serve Butter Sauce with steak or other meats of choice.

Family Favorite

Adam & Eve's Coffee Shop

8949 North US Highway 259
Broken Bow, OK 74728
580-494-6442
Find us on Facebook

Rise and shine with Adam & Eve's Coffee Shop. Adam & Eve's is a combination coffee shop and eatery serving up tasty breakfast sandwiches and sweets each morning as well as sandwiches, soups, baked potatoes, and salads at lunchtime. You can also enjoy lovely coffee and espresso all day, featuring flavors like white-chocolate mocha, salted caramel, vanilla, pumpkin, mocha, hazelnut, French vanilla, cinnamon, peppermint, English toffee, and Irish cream. The restaurant is also a great place to enjoy a variety of hot teas. At Adam & Eve's, you'll always leave satisfied.

Monday – Saturday: 7:00 am to 8:00 pm
Sunday: 7:00 am to 3:00 pm

Bagel Sandwich

1 sausage patty
1 egg
1 slice American cheese
1 plain bagel, halved

In a skillet over medium-high heat, cooked sausage patty until browned and crispy. In sausage fat, fry egg to desired doneness. To assemble sandwich, place sausage, egg and cheese on one bagel half and top with the other bagel half. Toast on a panini press until bagel is crispy and cheese is melted.

Restaurant Recipe

Iced Caramel Macchiato

2 pumps vanilla-flavored coffee syrup
4 pumps caramel-flavored coffee syrup
Milk
Ice
Shot of espresso

In a 16-ounce glass, combine syrups. Add milk until glass is half full. Add ice until glass is three-quarters full. Add espresso over top and enjoy.

Restaurant Recipe

THE Blue Rooster

The Blue Rooster

10235 North US Highway 259
Broken Bow, OK 74728
580-494-6361
www.blueroosterok.com
Find us on Facebook

Take a trip to Hochatown for The Blue Rooster. This quaint eatery serves fried chicken, fried farm-raised catfish, and sides galore, all made fresh to order. Popular menu items include the lightly breaded chicken strips, the fried fish basket with hushpuppies, and fried bologna sandwiches. The Blue Rooster also offers a variety of sides, from fried pickles to coleslaw. Enjoy your meal with a cold beer—domestic, import, or Oklahoma-brewed—and a fried pie for dessert. When the weather is nice, you can even enjoy your meal on the outdoor patio. Stop by for good food, good people, big porches, and live music.

Monday – Thursday: 11:00 am to 8:30 pm
Friday & Saturday: 11:00 am to 9:00 pm
Sunday: 10:30 am to 9:00 pm

Joyce Ann's Peach Pie

This is the perfect summer pie, courtesy of owner Suzie Carper's mother, Joyce Ann. It's sometimes served as a special dessert at The Blue Rooster.

1 cup sugar

2½ tablespoons cornstarch

1 (3-ounce) box cook-and-serve peach (or apricot) Jell-O

5 peaches, peeled and sliced, divided

1 teaspoon vanilla extract

1 (9-inch) frozen deep-dish pie crust, baked

Whipped cream for topping

In a saucepan, combine sugar and cornstarch; add 1½ cups water, stirring until smooth. Add Jell-O and ½ cup peaches; set over medium heat and stir until thickened. Add vanilla, then remove from heat to cool slightly. Add remaining peach slices to pie crust; pour filling over top. Cover with foil and refrigerate 2 to 4 hours. Serve with whipped cream.

Family Favorite

Hot Chicken Salad

A family favorite recipe sometimes served as a special at The Blue Rooster.

3 cups cooked cubed chicken breast

1½ cups diced celery

½ cup minced onion

½ cup sliced almonds

2 teaspoons lemon juice

1 teaspoon salt

Dash pepper

1 cup mayonnaise

1½ cups crushed Ruffles potato chips

1½ cups grated cheese mixture (half Cheddar, half Colby)

Preheat oven to 350°. In a large mixing bowl, combine chicken, celery, onion, almonds, lemon juice, salt and pepper. Add mayonnaise and toss until evenly coated. Transfer mixture to a 2-quart baking dish and top with chips and cheese. Bake 15 minutes until cheese is melted. Serves 8.

Family Favorite

GRATEFUL HEAD PIZZA OVEN

Grateful Head Pizza Oven & Tap Room

10251 North US Highway 259
Broken Bow, OK 74728
580-494-6030
www.gratefulheadpizza.com
Find us on Facebook

Grateful Head Pizza Oven & Tap Room began its journey in Hochatown. Built from the bones of an old abandoned schoolhouse, the restaurant quickly became the grooviest place to enjoy a pizza and a beer. Try tasty specialty pizzas, like the Psychedelic Supremo, Maui Waui, Pig Pen, Tree Hugger, Big Frank, Funky Chicken, and the Chelsea. You can also order a custom pizza that is tailored to your liking and personalized with your favorite toppings. Don't forget to sample extras, like the Cheese Styx brushed with garlic butter, the refreshing Shakedown Salad, or the Wings of Fire. Visit today for hot pizza, beer on tap, live music, and souvenirs.

Sunday – Thursday: 11:00 am to 9:00 pm
Friday & Saturday: 11:00 am to 10:00 pm

Quick Chicken & Rice Soup

3 (14.5-ounce) cans chicken stock
1½ cups quick-cooking rice
1 pound boneless, skinless chicken breasts, cut into ½-inch cubes
1½ teaspoons minced fresh ginger
1 tablespoon hot chile oil
1 tablespoon rice wine vinegar
1 bunch green onions, thinly sliced

In a large saucepan over high heat, bring chicken stock, rice and 3 cups water to a boil. Add chicken; reduce heat to medium-low. Cover and cook about 6 minutes or until rice is tender and chicken is white in center. Add ginger, chile oil, vinegar and green onions; cook 2 minutes more to blend flavors. Enjoy.

Local Favorite

Pepper Steak

1 (1- to 2-pound) package cube steak, sliced into strips
2 tablespoons oil
¼ cup chopped onion
1 clove garlic, minced
1 teaspoon salt
1 teaspoon pepper
1 beef bouillon cube
1 (15-ounce) can petite diced tomatoes
1 green bell pepper, sliced into thin strips
3 tablespoons flour
2 tablespoons soy sauce

Brown steak strips in oil over low heat about 10 to 15 minutes; add onion, garlic, salt and pepper. Dissolve bouillon cube in 1 cup boiling water; add to meat. Cover and simmer 25 minutes. Add tomatoes and bell pepper, then simmer 15 minutes more. Mix flour with ½ cup cold water and add soy sauce. Pour into meat, stirring slowly until thickened. Cook over low heat another 30 minutes.

Local Favorite

Hochatown BBQ

9123 North US Highway 259
Broken Bow, OK 74728
580-494-7301
www.hochatownbbq.com • Find us on Facebook

Located in the heart of Beavers Bend State Park, Hochatown BBQ serves up delicious barbecue in a quaint atmosphere. Enjoy classics like brisket, smoked turkey, pork, sausage, and hot links. Try the barbecue sandwich basket for tender barbecue smothered in Hochatown's original sauce and served with a side of your choice. You can also sample dinner plates featuring brisket, baby back ribs, catfish, and more. While there, stop for old-time photos, get a scoop at the ice cream parlor, or play eighteen holes of mini golf around an Old West town. Visit the gift shop for a souvenir of your visit. Hochatown BBQ will keep you coming back for more.

Daily: 10:30 am to 5:00 pm

Hochatown BBQ
Baked Beans

1 (117-ounce) can Bush's baked beans
¼ cup chopped onion
1 teaspoon mustard
¼ cup mild Hochatown BBQ sauce
¼ cup hot Hochatown BBQ sauce
¼ pound cooked brisket, chopped

In a large saucepan, combine beans, onion, mustard and barbecue sauces; stir until combined. Fold in brisket, then cook over low heat until heated through. Enjoy.

Restaurant Recipe

Hochatown BBQ Brisket

1 whole brisket
Hochatown BBQ Rub to taste
Hickory wood chips for smoking

Season both sides of brisket with rub; set aside. Preheat smoker to 225° and fill with hickory wood chips. When heated, place brisket in smoker; smoke 2½ hours. Remove brisket and set on a sheet of foil; partially wrap brisket, then add ½ cup water. Wrap brisket completely and place back in smoker for 5½ hours. Reduce heat to 165° and smoke 8 hours more. This brisket can't be beat!

Restaurant Recipe

Mountain Fork Brewery

89 North Lukfata Trail Road
Broken Bow, OK 74728
580-494-3233
www.mtforkbrewery.com • Find us on Facebook

Get ready to experience McCurtain County's finest when you visit Mountain Fork Brewery. Established in 2015, the brewery and restaurant offers handcrafted beer that pairs perfectly with mouthwatering meals. Well versed in beer craft, the brewery uses pristine water from the nearby Mountain Fork River in its brewing process. From a good source comes good beer. Patrons can also enjoy handcrafted burgers and handmade brick-oven pizzas. Before you leave, try the Salty Dog dessert, a rich chocolate cake combined with whipped cream, hot fudge, and salted caramel. Stop by Mountain Fork Brewery, where you can find easy-drinking, creatively crafted beer made with you in mind.

Sunday – Thursday: 11:00 am to 9:00 pm
Friday & Saturday: 11:00 am to 11:00 pm

Mountain Fork Burger

4 to 6 ounces fresh ground chuck
Salt to taste
Pepper to taste
Minced garlic to taste
Cornmeal-dusted kaiser bun
Sliced cheese of choice
Sliced toppings of choice (tomatoes, lettuce, onion, etc.)

Form ground chuck into a ball; place on a heated flattop grill and season with salt, pepper and garlic. Press flat with spatula; cook 3 to 5 minutes or until cooked through. Cut patty from grill, leaving crust. Assemble burger on kaiser bun with cheese and toppings of choice. Enjoy.

Restaurant Recipe

Pepperoni Pizza

10 to 12 ounces pizza dough
House tomato sauce as needed
Crumbled goat cheese as needed
Sliced pepperoni as needed

With floured hands, toss and stretch dough to form pizza crust; lay on a lightly floured baking peel. Add tomato sauce, leaving a 1-inch border around the edge. Top with goat cheese, then add pepperoni. Slip pizza into brick oven using baking peel. Bake until cheese is melted and crust is puffed and browned, about 1½ to 2 minutes. Carefully slide pizza onto peel, remove from oven, slice and enjoy.

Restaurant Recipe

Rolling Fork Takery

5 Coho Road
Broken Bow, OK 74728
580-494-7655
www.rollingforktakery.com
Find us on Facebook

Rolling Fork Takery believes if we go back to our roots, we can eat good and feel good. For this reason, the owners returned to Hochatown, back to the lands of their ancestors, with a fresh take on some very old and time-honored family traditions. "Back to our roots," to the owners of Rolling Fork Takery, means a return to nature, to a way of preparing and sharing foods like their grandparents did. It is this organic life, filled with generous hearts and vivid heritage, that Rolling Fork Takery wants to share with customers. When you visit, you'll not only take away wholesome, delicious food but also a taste of local culture and character that shape a unique approach to life.

A Takery Concept "Farm-to-Fork" Fresh Foods Grill & Deli

Open Year-Round
Tuesday – Sunday: 11:00 am

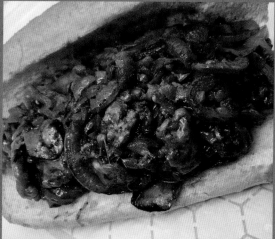

Rolling Fork Sliders

**1¼ pounds (20 ounces) certified
Angus ground beef**
Sea salt and pepper to taste
2 white onions
4 slices American cheese, halved
Mayonnaise to taste
8 Hawaiian slider buns, lightly toasted

Using a kitchen scale, separate beef into 2.5-ounce portions, forming each into a 3-inch patty. Lightly season each side with salt and pepper, then transfer to a grill. Grill patties over open flame to desired doneness, then transfer to a baking sheet. Meanwhile, dice onions, sprinkle with salt and sauté in a skillet over medium-high heat until caramelized. Top each patty with onions and half a slice of cheese; broil in oven until cheese begins to melt. Dollop mayonnaise onto buns, then assemble sliders. Makes 4 servings of 2 sliders per person.

Restaurant Recipe

Shuck Me

83 North Lukfata Trail Road
Broken Bow, OK 74728
580-494-FISH (3474)
www.shuckme.net • Find us on Facebook

Come on out to Shuck Me, a seafood restaurant that serves tasty food to Broken Bow locals and visitors alike. The menu features a variety of handmade cocktails, fresh oysters, and appetizers. Choose from fried fish, shrimp, chicken, or oyster baskets as well as grilled fish plates, salads, boiled seafood, homemade soups, burgers, fish tacos, po'boys, and more. Shuck Me also hosts live music and other events, so you can enjoy a show with your meal. You don't want to miss it.

Call for Seasonal Hours

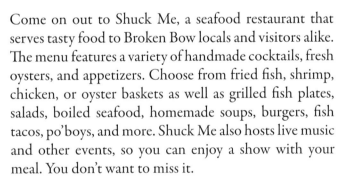

Crab Delights

1 cup fresh crabmeat
2 tablespoons mayonnaise
1 teaspoon curry powder
¼ teaspoon salt
⅛ teaspoon pepper
½ teaspoon Worcestershire sauce

In a bowl, mix all ingredients together, taking care not to break crabmeat. Serve on crackers.

Restaurant Recipe

Shrimp Salad

1 pound shrimp
Zatarain's crab boil (or crab boil of choice) as needed
4 eggs, boiled and chopped
4 stalks celery, chopped
Salad dressing of choice as needed
Lettuce leaves for serving
Crackers for serving

In a large stockpot, boil shrimp in crab boil; strain out, peel and chop. In a bowl, stir together shrimp, eggs, celery and enough salad dressing to coat. Serve Shrimp Salad on lettuce leaves with crackers.

Restaurant Recipe

June's Restaurant

123 South Broadway Street
Checotah, OK 74426
918-473-2356
junes-restaurant.business.site • Find us on Facebook

Welcome to June's Restaurant, the perfect place to find the best home cooking in Checotah. Be sure to try the delicious chicken-fried steak or a handmade quarter-pound burger made with fresh ground beef. The restaurant also serves a variety of appetizers, such as fried mushrooms and cheese balls, as well as refreshing salads and a soup of the day if you're in the mood for a lighter course. The homemade desserts are made fresh daily, so don't forget to ask your server for a sample of sweetness. Stop by June's Restaurant for comfort food in a down-home atmosphere.

Monday – Saturday: 11:00 am to 9:00 pm

Cowboy Stew

1½ pounds ground beef
½ onion, chopped
Fajita seasoning to taste
4 (10.75-ounce) cans minestrone soup
1 (15-ounce) can ranch-style beans
½ (10-ounce) can Rotel tomatoes

In a large saucepan over medium-high heat, brown beef. When nearly browned, add onion; stir constantly, cooking until onion is translucent. Drain fat, then stir in fajita seasoning. Add minestrone; fill empty cans about halfway with water and add to saucepan. Stir in beans and Rotel; reduce heat to low and simmer about 20 minutes. Enjoy.

Restaurant Recipe

Goulash

2 pounds ground beef
1 teaspoon onion salt
1 teaspoon garlic salt
1 dash pepper
1 onion, chopped
1 green bell pepper, chopped
**2 (14.5-ounce) cans diced
fire-roasted tomatoes**
1 pound cooked elbow noodles
3 (14-ounce) cans tomato sauce

In a large saucepan over medium-high heat, combine beef, onion salt, garlic salt and pepper; cook, stirring occasionally, until beef is nearly browned. Add onion and bell pepper, cooking until onion is translucent and bell pepper is tender. Add tomatoes, elbow noodles and tomato sauce. Reduce heat to low and simmer 10 minutes until heated through. Enjoy.

Restaurant Recipe

The Farmstead

117 South Franklin Street
Colbert, OK 74733
580-296-2201
www.thefarmstead.biz • Find us on Facebook

Ronnie and Trena Wines both grew up working on farms. Ronnie spent most summers of his youth working in fields, while Trena's grandparents taught her about the farming process from field to market. The two opened The Farmstead with a vision: to offer customers fresh food that balances gluten-free, dairy-free, and vegetarian options with traditional home-style favorites, all without sacrificing taste. The restaurant emphasizes the importance of farm-to-table meals by sourcing produce from local farmers whenever possible. Seasonal and daily specials are also offered, and customers can also purchase local honey, jelly, and other items from area vendors. Visit The Farmstead for fresh food and scratch-made pies.

Tuesday – Friday: 11:00 am to 9:00 pm
Saturday: 9:00 am to 9:00 pm
Sunday: 9:00 am to 2:00 pm

Avocado BLT

A Farmstead top seller.

2 tablespoons butter
2 pieces Texas toast
3 slices bacon
**1 tablespoon Farmstead mayonnaise
(or mayo with herbs)**
1 leaf lettuce
1 to 2 slices tomato
½ avocado, peeled and sliced

In a skillet over medium heat, melt butter; add Texas toast, toasting each side. In another skillet, fry bacon until crisp. Dress toast with mayonnaise, lettuce, tomato and avocado. Remove bacon from skillet and pat off excess grease with paper towel. Add bacon to sandwich and enjoy.

Restaurant Recipe

Buttermilk Pie

This recipe for this pie belonged to Trena's great-grandmother Martha Cantrell Davis, born 1878.

2 cups sugar
2 tablespoons all-purpose flour
2 tablespoons cornmeal
3 eggs
1 stick butter, melted
½ cup buttermilk
1 teaspoon vanilla extract
1 (9-inch) frozen pie crust, thawed
Ground nutmeg for sprinkling

Preheat oven to 425°. In a bowl, mix sugar, flour and cornmeal. In another bowl, mix eggs, butter, buttermilk and vanilla. Gradually mix dry ingredients into wet ingredients, stirring well after each addition to prevent lumps. Pour filling into pie shell and sprinkle with nutmeg. Bake 10 minutes, then reduce heat to 300°. Bake 30 minutes or until filling no longer jiggles.

Family Favorite

SMOKIN JOES Rib Ranch

3165 Jollyville Road
Davis, OK 73030
580-369-2818
www.smokinjoesribranch.com • Find us on Facebook

Smokin' Joe's Rib Ranch began serving its legendary barbecue when Joe Wells decided he needed a new hobby. Joe began serving barbecue in a gas station, and the business quickly grew. Soon, Joe's family was helping him out a couple days a week, and before long, the operation became a full-fledged restaurant. The Wells family smokes their meats over hickory all day every day to keep up with the significant demand. The primo barbecue and ribs are an offer you simply can't refuse. The restaurant stays busy, so come get in line. One diner described Smokin' Joe's barbecue as "slap yo mama good," so it's definitely worth the wait.

Monday & Tuesday: 11:00 am to 8:00 pm
Thursday – Saturday: 11:00 am to 8:00 pm

Smokin' Joe's Coleslaw

5 pounds diced green cabbage
4 ounces shredded purple cabbage
4 ounces shredded carrot
1 Granny Smith apple, diced
2 cups mayonnaise
1 cup sugar
½ cup apple cider vinegar

In a large bowl, toss together green cabbage, purple cabbage, carrots and apple; set aside. In a small bowl, combine mayonnaise, sugar and vinegar; pour over cabbage mixture and stir to coat. Transfer to an airtight container and refrigerate at least 1 hour before serving.

Restaurant Recipe

Smokin' Joe's Potato Salad

5 pounds Idaho potatoes
3¼ cups mayonnaise
1 cup chopped dill pickles
¼ cup pickle juice
1 cup chopped onion
2 tablespoons salt
2 tablespoons pepper

Wash potatoes thoroughly; slice into ¼-inch-thick slices. Add potatoes to a large stockpot, cover with water and bring to a boil; lower heat and simmer 13 to 15 minutes until potatoes are cooked through but firm. Drain potatoes and place in a large pan; mash to coarse consistency. Stir in remaining ingredients; cool 10 to 15 minutes. Transfer to an airtight container and refrigerate until ready to serve.

Restaurant Recipe

Eufaula, OK   Est. 2000

Kassey Weaver Photography

E's Hideaway

134 North Main Street
Eufaula, OK 74432
918-967-9000
www.eshidewayrestaurantncatering.com
Find us on Facebook

Great food and company await you at E's Hideaway, a restaurant and catering business serving the Stigler and Eufaula communities since 2000. Once operated out of a shop behind chef Eric Sutherland's parents' store, the eatery later moved to a bespoke building in Stigler in April 2014. By March 2019, E's Hideaway had outgrown the space. Chef Eric and his wife, Amanda, continue operations at E's temporary location, 224 North Main Street. Just down the street, a remodel is underway in a beautiful historical building—E's Hideaway's new permanent location, slated to open December 2019. Join chef Eric and Amanda as they embark on this new chapter for E's Hideaway.

Lunch:
Tuesday – Sunday: 11:00 am to 2:30 pm
Dinner:
Tuesday – Thursday: 4:30 pm to 9:00 pm
Friday & Saturday: 4:30 pm to 10:00 pm

Molasses-Marinated Pork

Recipe by chef Eric Sutherland.

1 (2- to 3-pound) pork tenderloin
6 ounces molasses
4 cups water
3 tablespoons granulated garlic
4 tablespoons salt

Clean silver skin from tenderloin. In a large bowl, whisk remaining ingredients; marinate tenderloin 45 minutes to 1 hour. Place in smoker 10 minutes, then sear on all sides in a skillet over medium-high heat. Transfer to a baking dish and bake at 350° for 30 minutes or until internal temperature reaches 160°.

Dried Cranberry & Pecan Relish:

1 cup dried cranberries
¼ cup orange juice
¼ cup pecans

In a saucepan, simmer cranberries and orange juice until juice has evaporated. Stir in pecans. Garnish sliced and plated tenderloin with relish.

Restaurant Recipe

Sandy's Amazing Carrot Cake

Recipe by Amanda Sutherland in memory of Sandy Sutherland.

2 to 3 cups shredded carrot
2 cups sugar
4 eggs
1½ cups vegetable oil
2 cups all-purpose flour
3 teaspoons ground cinnamon
2 teaspoons baking soda
1 teaspoon salt
2 tablespoons vanilla extract

Preheat oven to 375°. In a mixing bowl, combine all ingredients and mix. Divide batter between 3 (9-inch) greased and floured cake pans; bake 30 minutes. Cool.

Cream Cheese Frosting:

1½ sticks butter
12 ounces cream cheese, softened
1½ pounds powdered sugar

In a bowl, beat butter and cream cheese with a handheld electric mixer until combined. Beat in powdered sugar until smooth. Assemble cooled cake layers, frosting between the layers and over the outside.

Restaurant Recipe

Southern Belle Restaurant

821 Highway 59 North
Heavener, OK 74937
918-653-4458
Find us on Facebook

Southern Belle Restaurant is located inside a restored 1905-dated railcar. Despite its small size, the restaurant is quite roomy inside and capable of hosting about fifty diners at once. This lovely little restaurant serves the most amazing, savory home cooking. Southern Belle Restaurant is famous for its Southern Belle chicken, boneless chicken strips that are marinated, breaded, deep-fried, and served with a side of the restaurant's famous house dipping sauce. You'll also enjoy tasty steaks, burgers, fish, sandwiches, and pork chops, all prepared in a down-home fashion. Don't forget to save room for dessert. A slice of delicious homemade pie is the perfect way to end your visit.

Monday & Tuesday: 11:00 am to 8:00 pm
Thursday – Saturday: 11:00 am to 9:00 pm
Sunday: 11:00 am to 2:00 pm

Broccoli & Rice Casserole

2 cups uncooked rice
1 tablespoon butter
½ onion, chopped
1 (10-ounce) box frozen chopped broccoli, thawed
1 (10.5-ounce) can cream of chicken soup
1 (15-ounce) jar Kraft Cheez Whiz

Preheat oven to 350°. Cook rice per package directions; set aside. In a saucepan over medium heat, melt butter and add onion; sauté until translucent. Add broccoli and cook 2 minutes or until slightly tender; stir in rice. Mix in soup and Cheez Whiz until combined. Transfer mixture to a 9x13-inch casserole dish and bake 30 minutes.

Family Favorite

Parmesan Chicken Breasts

¾ cup melted butter
1½ teaspoons Dijon mustard
1 clove garlic, crushed
1½ teaspoons Worcestershire sauce
2½ cups breadcrumbs
1 cup grated Parmesan cheese
½ cup grated Swiss cheese
2 to 3 tablespoons chopped fresh parsley
1 teaspoon salt
8 to 10 boneless, skinless chicken breasts

Preheat oven to 350°. In a bowl, mix butter, mustard, garlic and Worcestershire; set aside. In another bowl, mix breadcrumbs, cheeses, parsley and salt. Dip chicken in butter mixture, then dredge in breadcrumb mixture. Transfer to a greased 9x13-inch roasting pan. Drizzle remaining butter mixture over chicken, then bake 1½ hours.

Family Favorite

Pete's Place

120 Southwest 8th Street
Krebs, OK 74554
918-423-2042
www.petes.org • Find us on Facebook

The spicy bouquet of authentic Italian cooking wafting from Pete's Place has been luring travelers through the blackjack-covered hills of southeast Oklahoma since 1925. Four generations later, not much has changed. The restaurant still operates under the same family, at the same location, using the same traditional Italian recipes that made Pete's Place famous. The Choc beer is made with the same old recipe passed down through generations, though with one difference—it's now legal. Today, Joe and Kathy Prichard carry on the same family tradition, serving up great Italian food and handcrafted beer. When they say you're invited to their house for dinner, they mean it!

Monday – Thursday: 11:00 am to 9:00 pm
Friday & Saturday: 11:00 am to 10:00 pm
Sunday: 11:00 am to 8:00 pm

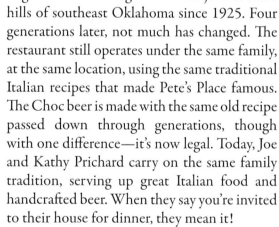

Meatballs

1 pound lean ground beef
½ pound ground veal
½ pound ground pork
2 eggs
1 cup grated fresh Pecorino Romano cheese
1½ tablespoons chopped fresh Italian parsley
½ clove garlic, minced
Salt and pepper to taste
2 cups breadcrumbs
Lukewarm water as needed
1 cup olive oil

In a large bowl, combine beef, veal and pork. Add eggs, cheese, parsley, garlic and salt and pepper; mix together by hand until combined. Mix in breadcrumbs, then slowly mix in water until mixture is moist yet still holds together if rolled into a ball; shape mixture into meatballs and place on a baking sheet. In a large skillet, heat olive oil to 325°. Fry meatballs in batches until browned and crisp, turning occasionally to ensure even browning. Drain on paper towels and enjoy.

Restaurant Recipe

Pasta e Fagioli (Pasta & White Bean Soup)

6 tablespoons extra virgin olive oil plus more for drizzling
2 cups chopped onion
1 cup chopped carrot
1 cup chopped celery
8 cups chicken stock
5 cups cooked white beans
2 (14.5-ounce) cans diced tomatoes
2 cups uncooked ditalini pasta
2 green onions, chopped
Salt and pepper to taste

In a heavy-bottom stockpot over medium heat, combine olive oil, onion, carrot and celery; sauté until vegetables are soft. Add stock, beans and tomatoes; reduce heat and simmer 1 hour or until aromatic. Add pasta and bring to a boil; cook until pasta is tender. Ladle soup into bowls, drizzle with olive oil and top with green onions. Add salt and pepper to taste.

Family Favorite

ROSEANNA'S
italian food

205 E WASHINGTON . KREBS, OK. 918-423-2055

205 East Washington
Krebs, OK 74554
918-423-2055
www.roseannas.com
Find us on Facebook

Frank Prichard had long dreamed of opening an Italian restaurant. In 1975, he realized his dream with the help of his wife, Rose Ann, and their children. The carry-out restaurant enjoyed popular success but shuttered in early 1978 while Frank recuperated from heart surgery and a broken leg. The next year, the family purchased an old home, and after a long remodel, Roseanna's Italian Food opened its doors in 1980. Frank worked hard, proudly serving customers until he passed in 1988. Rose Ann passed in 2008, leaving their children, grandchildren, and industrious work staff to carry on their dream. Handmade gnocchi, ravioli, and lasagna are a few comfort food dishes that bring customers back time and time again.

Tuesday & Wednesday:
11:00 am to 8:00 pm
Thursday – Saturday: 11:00 am to 9:00 pm
Sunday: 11:30 am to 2:30 pm

Gnocchi

6 cups fresh mashed potatoes
3 cups all-purpose flour
3 teaspoons salt
4 eggs

In a mixing bowl, combine all ingredients except eggs, mixing until combined. Add eggs; mix well. Turn out dough onto a well-floured countertop and gently knead, working in more flour if too soft. Cut off a piece of dough and roll into a "snake" about ¾ inch in diameter; cut into 1-inch pieces. Roll and press into a gnocchi board or a fork to make ridges. In a large stockpot, bring salted water to a boil. Drop gnocchi in, and after they float to the top, cook 5 to 6 minutes. You may also freeze uncooked gnocchi on a baking sheet for later use. Enjoy with tomato sauce, butter sauce or other sauce of choice.

Restaurant Recipe

Chithone

A type of quiche made during the Easter holiday. Different families have different spellings.

1 (9x13-inch) fresh pie crust
14 eggs
3 cups diced ham
3 cups diced Muenster cheese
1 teaspoon granulated garlic

Preheat oven to 350°. Line a 9x13-inch baking dish with pie crust. In a large bowl, beat eggs. Mix in remaining ingredients, then pour mixture into pie crust. Bake 45 minutes to 1 hour. Serve hot or cold.

Family Recipe

Angel's Diner

1402 South George Nigh Expressway
McAlester, OK 74501
918-423-2633
www.angels50sdiner.com • Find us on Facebook

Angel's Diner is McAlester's hidden gem for food, folks, and fun. At Angel's, you'll enjoy an experience that transports you back in time to 1950s-style dining, complete with jukebox hits from a bygone era. Guests will enjoy a traditional American breakfast every morning that features omelets, pancakes, French toast, and more. Lunch at Angel's is always special, with American classics like burgers, fries, and soda. The diner also offers a selection of sandwiches and blue plate specials. For dinner, dine on ribeye, fried catfish, chicken-fried steak, and more. Visit Angel's Diner for great food, attentive service, and a blast from the past.

Monday – Saturday:
7:00 am to 9:00 pm
Sunday:
8:00 am to 3:00 pm

Beef Biscuit Roll

1 pound ground chuck
½ cup chopped onion
2 tablespoons chopped green bell pepper
2 tablespoons mayonnaise
2 tablespoons ketchup
¾ teaspoon salt
⅛ teaspoon pepper
¼ teaspoon celery salt
1 egg, beaten
3¼ cups biscuit mix
1⅔ cups milk, divided
1 (10.75-ounce) can cream
of chicken soup

Preheat oven to 375°. In a bowl, combine chuck, onion, bell pepper, mayonnaise, ketchup, salt, pepper, celery salt and egg; mix well. In a 2-quart bowl, mix biscuit mix and 1 cup milk with a fork to form a dough. Turn out on a lightly floured surface; roll or pat dough into a 12x15-inch rectangle. Spread beef mixture evenly over dough surface. Roll up like you would a jelly roll. Cut into 12 slices about 1½ inches thick. Place slices in a greased baking pan; bake 25 minutes. In a saucepan over medium heat combine soup and remailing ⅔ cup milk; bring to a boil, stirring often. Pour over rolls as you serve them.

Local Favorite

Baked Spareribs

2 slabs pork spareribs
½ cup barbecue sauce plus
more for basting
Salt and pepper

Preheat oven to 300°. Place spareribs in a Dutch oven, cover with water and bring to a boil; boil 10 minutes. Drain water and transfer ribs to an 11x13-inch baking dish. Add ½ cup water to bottom of dish. Cover ribs with barbecue sauce. Roast 2 hours or until tender, occasionally basting with more barbecue sauce. Season with salt and pepper before serving.

Local Favorite

Warehouse Willy's

300 Dewey Avenue
Poteau, OK 74953
918-649-3400
Find us on Facebook

Located in historic downtown Poteau, Warehouse Willy's serves up restaurant-style meals in a pub-style setting. Guests will enjoy a relaxed atmosphere that is low-lit for comfort with exciting pops of light from neon signs. Signs of all kinds adorn the walls, from road signs to license plates. The restaurant serves everything from steak and chicken to shrimp and

burgers. It is truly a steakhouse unlike any other. Drop by Warehouse Willy's to sample unique twists on traditional dinners.

Lunch:
Tuesday, Wednesday, & Friday: 11:00 am to 2:00 pm
Dinner:
Tuesday – Saturday: 5:00 pm to 9:00 pm

Fried Cabbage & Cherry Tomatoes

6 slices hickory-smoked bacon
1 cup chicken stock
1 head cabbage, chopped
2 tablespoons oil
½ (1-ounce) envelope onion soup mix
1 tablespoon Willy's steak powder
1 red onion, diced
1 pint cherry tomatoes, halved

In a large skillet over medium heat, cook bacon until crisp; remove from skillet and drain on paper towels. Deglaze skillet with chicken stock. Add cabbage, oil, soup mix and steak powder; cook until cabbage is crisp. Add onion and cook until soft. Crumble bacon and add to skillet; cook 5 minutes. Add cherry tomatoes. Cover and cook 5 minutes. Enjoy.

Restaurant Recipe

No-Milk Mash

4 potatoes
Chicken stock for boiling
½ teaspoon sea salt
½ cup plus 1 tablespoon butter
1 teaspoon Willy's steak powder
½ (1-ounce) packet ranch dressing mix
½ cup sour cream
Salt and pepper to taste

Peel and cut potatoes into 1-inch cubes; place in a saucepan and cover with chicken stock. Stir in sea salt and 1 tablespoon butter; boil until potatoes are soft, then strain out. Add potatoes to a large mixing bowl with steak powder, ranch dressing mix, sour cream and remaining ½ cup butter. Mix with a handheld electric mixer set to medium speed until smooth. Adjust consistency with additional butter and sour cream as needed. Add salt and pepper. Enjoy.

Restaurant Recipe

Debbie's Bus Station Café

411 East Broadway Avenue
Seminole, OK 74868
405-382-9997
Find us on Facebook

Debbie's Bus Station Café is an acclaimed destination in Seminole featuring an appetizing menu with delicious dishes. Visitors come for the quality food and stay for the helpful service. Prices might be lower than average, but at Debbie's Bus Station Café, that doesn't mean you'll be sacrificing quality. For breakfast, dine on classics like eggs, bacon, hotcakes, waffles, and biscuits. When lunch rolls around, you'll enjoy tasty entrées like chicken-fried steak, fried catfish, steak sandwiches, cheeseburgers, and so much more. Between the mouthwatering fare and the friendly service, you'll be a regular at Debbie's Bus Station Café before you know it.

Monday – Thursday: 6:00 am to 2:00 pm
Friday: 6:00 am to 8:00 pm
Saturday: 6:00 am to 4:00 pm

Quick Biscuits

2 cups all-purpose flour
plus more for rolling

2 teaspoons baking powder

1 teaspoon salt

1 stick butter, softened

Milk as needed

Preheat oven to 400°. In a mixing bowl, whisk together dry ingredients; cut in butter. Stir in milk as needed until dough is sticky. Turn out onto floured surface and sprinkle with flour; press down and fold in half twice. Roll out to desired thickness and cut out biscuits, arranging them on a baking sheet. Bake 15 minutes or until risen and browned on top.

Family Favorite

Chicken Soup

2 to 3 chicken breasts

2 stalks celery, chopped

1 onion, chopped

2 cloves garlic, chopped

3 carrots, sliced

2 to 3 potatoes, diced

1 green bell pepper, deseeded
and chopped

1 to 2 hot peppers, deseeded
and chopped

2 cups peeled and diced tomatoes

To a large stockpot, add chicken breasts. Cover with water and boil until cooked through. Remove chicken from stockpot and cube; set aside. Strain broth, reserving 4½ to 5½ cups; add reserved broth back to pot. Set pot over medium heat, then add all vegetables except tomatoes. Cook until vegetables are tender, then stir in tomatoes and chicken. Lower heat to medium-low, then cook until heated through. Enjoy.

Family Favorite

REAL BEEF JERKY
Robertson's
HAMS

11276 North Highway 99
Seminole, OK 74868
405-382-0555
www.robertsons-hams.com • Find us on Facebook

Robertson's Hams has been serving sugar-cured, hickory-smoked hams, turkey, beef jerky, smoked sausage, and other smoked meats since 1946. The ham house seasons and cures its meats for a week before slicing, smoking, and packaging for customers. Robertson's also offers customers in-store dining. Try the Big'un, a six-ounce sandwich with your choice of up to three smoked meats. If you're in the mood for something classic, you can't go wrong with the Reuben. You can also complement your meal with your choice of two sides, potato salad or potato chips, and a range of bottled drinks, fountain drinks, coffee, or tea. Stop by Robertson's—a name you can trust.

Monday – Thursday & Saturday: 8:00 am to 5:30 pm
Friday: 8:00 am to 6:00 pm

Barbecue Sausage

Try this for a really quick and delicious meal. You can also quarter the sausage and follow the same instructions with a slow cooker instead of an oven, if desired. This is a very simple meal, but it is quick and easy when there isn't much time to prepare something larger.

2 pounds Robertson's smoked pork sausage
Robertson's barbecue sauce as needed

Preheat oven to 325°. With a sharp knife, slice sausage into ¾-inch-thick pieces. Add sausage to a 9x13-inch baking dish, then cover with barbecue sauce. Bake 15 minutes.

Restaurant Recipe

Bacon Wraps

10 slices bread
1 (10.5-ounce) can cream of mushroom soup
10 slices Robertson's cured and smoked bacon, halved

Preheat oven to 400°. Cut crusts off of bread slices. Spread soup on one side of a bread slice; roll up bread slice with soup side on inside. Wrap each end with a half strip bacon, then secure with a toothpick. Repeat for each slice bread. Arrange wraps on a greased baking sheet and bake 30 to 45 minutes. (Baking time will vary based on your oven and the leanness of the bacon.)

Restaurant Recipe

Fat Bully's by the Lake

3133 Chickasaw Trail
Sulphur, OK 73086
580-622-5616
fat-bullys.business.site • Find us on Facebook

Fat Bully's by the Lake is best known for the three B's: burgers, beer, and bikes. All of the restaurant's burgers start with a fresh, certified-Angus half-pound patty. From there, Fat Bully's offers a variety of custom burgers, from the Vroom Vroom Shroom burger to the Ducati burger. Guests will also enjoy tasty sides, like chips and salsa, broke spokes, fire fries, and more. Don't forget that several delicious salads are available, as well, if burgers aren't your vice. Fat Bully's is the perfect scenic destination to enjoy a fun, family-friendly environment and great burgers.

Friday & Saturday: 11:00 am to 8:00 pm
Sunday: 11:00 am to 7:00 pm

Chicken Marsala

2 tablespoons olive oil
½ cup plus 1 tablespoon all-purpose flour, divided
4 boneless, skinless chicken breasts
Salt and pepper to taste
3 small shallots, chopped
1 cup sliced chestnut mushrooms
½ cup marsala wine
1 cup chicken stock
Chopped fresh parsley for topping

To a deep skillet over medium-high heat, add olive oil. To a shallow bowl, add ½ cup flour. Cover chicken breasts with plastic wrap and pound with a meat mallet to an even ½-inch thickness. Sprinkle breasts with salt and pepper on each side, then dredge in flour in shallow bowl; fry about 5 minutes in olive oil until golden, flipping once. (Do not overcook; chicken breasts will cook quickly as they are thin.) Remove chicken and set aside. To same skillet, add shallots; cook over low heat 2 to 3 minutes. Add mushrooms and salt and pepper, then sauté 5 minutes. Stir in remaining 1 tablespoon flour, then cook 1 minute longer. Add wine and increase heat to medium. Add stock and bring to a boil; reduce heat to a gentle simmer, then return chicken to skillet. Cook until chicken is heated through and sauce has thickened to desired consistency. Serve sprinkled with parsley and your side dish of choice.

Family Favorite

Dorito Casserole

1½ pounds lean ground beef
¼ cup chopped onion
1 (1-ounce) packet taco seasoning
1 cup salsa verde
1 (10.5-ounce) can cream of chicken soup
1 cup sour cream
1 cup shredded Cheddar cheese
1 (9.75-ounce) bag nacho cheese Doritos, crushed
1 cup shredded Colby Jack cheese

Preheat oven to 350°. To a large skillet over medium heat, add beef and onion; cook until meat is browned and onion is translucent, then drain fat. Add taco seasoning and 1 cup water; stir until combined. Cook over medium heat 3 minutes or until thickened; remove from heat. Stir in salsa, soup and sour cream until combined. Stir in Cheddar until melted. In a 9x13-inch casserole dish, layer a third of the Doritos, then top with half of beef mixture; repeat layering once. Top with remaining third of Doritos and Colby Jack. Cover with greased foil and bake 25 minutes; remove foil and bake 20 minutes more.

Family Favorite

The Rusty Nail Winery

218 West Muskogee Avenue
Sulphur, OK 73086
580-622-8466
www.rustynailwinery.com • Find us on Facebook, Twitter & Instagram

The Rusty Nail Winery is a winery, tasting room, gift shop, and bistro located in Chickasaw Country. This family-friendly attraction offers tourists and locals alike a place to sip, taste, and relax. While visiting, select the perfect bottle of wine to take home, explore the unique gift shop, or sample tasty foods from The Rusty Nail Bistro. The winery specializes in wines made from high-quality varietals and starts with juice instead of grapes, resulting in a wide variety of wines, from bold reds to crisp whites to fruit and dessert wines. Whether you're a wine novice or wine expert, your experience will be truly unique.

Tuesday – Saturday:
Noon to 8:00 pm

Broccoli–Potato Soup

2 cups chopped red potatoes

1 (14-ounce) can chicken stock

3 cups small broccoli florets

2 cups milk

2 cups shredded Gouda cheese plus more for topping

3 tablespoons all-purpose flour

Salt and pepper to taste

In a large lidded stockpot, combine potatoes and stock; bring to a boil, reduce to a simmer, cover and cook 8 minutes. When soft, mash potatoes slightly, then stir in broccoli and milk; bring to a simmer again. In a medium bowl, toss together cheese and flour; gradually add to soup, stirring after each addition, until cheese is melted. Season with salt and pepper. Ladle into shallow bowls and top with additional cheese before serving.

Restaurant Recipe

Spinach–Artichoke Dip

1 (16-ounce) bag frozen spinach, thawed

1 (14-ounce) can artichoke hearts

1 (8-ounce) package cream cheese, softened

¼ cup mayonnaise

¼ cup sour cream

½ teaspoon red pepper flakes

⅛ teaspoon garlic powder

Salt and pepper to taste

⅛ cup grated Parmesan cheese

2 tablespoons Italian seasoning

1 cup shredded 3-cheese blend

Rinse and drain spinach and artichokes; set aside. In a large bowl, combine cream cheese, mayonnaise, sour cream, spices, Parmesan and Italian seasoning; mix until combined. Fold in spinach and artichokes; transfer to an oven-safe baking dish. Sprinkle with 3-cheese blend, then broil until cheese is bubbly and browned.

Restaurant Recipe

Pam's Hateful Hussy Diner

304 Dallas Street
Talihina, OK 74571
918-567-2051

Pam's Hateful Hussy Diner is an iconic eatery in southeastern Oklahoma. Named after owner Pam Lewis, the diner got its name one busy day when a patron asked Pam for coffee while she had her hands full. She responded, "You've been coming in here long enough. You know where the coffee is. Get it yourself." The patron replied, "You old, hateful hussy," and the name stuck. The diner serves delicious home-style country food made fresh daily, ranging from breakfast items in the morning to tasty lunch dishes when afternoon rolls around. Don't leave without trying the chicken-fried steak, fresh vegetables, and a homemade dessert. Don't miss this Talihina staple.

Monday – Saturday: 5:00 am to 9:00 pm
Sunday: 7:00 am to 2:00 pm

Chicken–Fried Steak

1½ cups whole milk

2 large eggs, beaten

2 cups all-purpose flour

2 teaspoons seasoned salt

Pepper to taste

¾ teaspoon paprika

¼ teaspoon cayenne pepper

3 pounds cube steak

Kosher salt to taste

½ cup vegetable oil

1 tablespoon butter

In a bowl, whisk milk and eggs. In another bowl, whisk together flour and seasonings. Sprinkle steak on both sides with kosher salt and pepper; dredge in flour. Dip steak in egg mixture; dredge steak in flour once again, coating well. Set aside; repeat with remaining steaks. Heat oil in a large skillet over medium heat, then add butter. A few at a time, cook steaks 2 minutes each side until edges start to turn golden brown. Rest on paper towels.

Local Favorite

Gravy

¼ cup reserved used vegetable oil

⅓ cup all-purpose flour

3 to 4 cups whole milk as needed

½ teaspoon seasoned salt

Pepper to taste

To a skillet, add oil; heat over medium-low heat. When hot, sprinkle flour evenly over surface; whisk until a paste forms. If too greasy, add more flour; if too clumpy, add more oil. Continue cooking, whisking constantly, until roux becomes a deep golden brown. Add milk, whisking constantly. Add seasoned salt and pepper; cook 5 to 10 minutes, whisking constantly, until smooth and thick. Add more milk if gravy becomes too thick. Serve over Chicken-Fried Steak.

Local Favorite

The Rock House

52060 Blackjack Ridge Drive
Talihina, OK 74571
918-567-3577
TheROCKHouse.US • Find us on Facebook

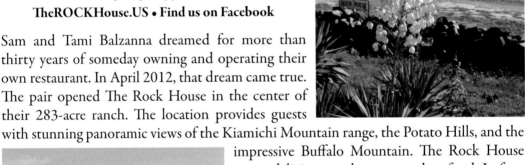

Sam and Tami Balzanna dreamed for more than thirty years of someday owning and operating their own restaurant. In April 2012, that dream came true. The pair opened The Rock House in the center of their 283-acre ranch. The location provides guests with stunning panoramic views of the Kiamichi Mountain range, the Potato Hills, and the

impressive Buffalo Mountain. The Rock House serves delicious steak, pasta, and seafood. In fact, it's well known for its aged hand-carved Angus steaks, Maryland-style crab cakes, fresh salads, pastas, and house-made rolls. You are guaranteed to be delighted from the first sip of wine to the last bite of the house favorite, carrot cake.

Sunday & Thursday: 4:00 pm to 8:00 pm
Friday & Saturday: 4:00 pm to 8:30 pm

Reservations Required

Carbonara

1 pound uncooked spaghetti
¼ pound prosciutto, chopped
¼ cup extra virgin olive oil
1 teaspoon red pepper flakes
5 to 6 cloves garlic
(or 8 to 9...who's counting?), minced
½ cup pinot grigio wine
2 egg yolks
¼ cup freshly grated Romano cheese
¼ cup freshly grated Parmesan cheese
Salt and pepper to taste
Chopped fresh parsley for garnish

In a stockpot, cook spaghetti per package directions. Brown prosciutto in olive oil in a nonstick skillet over medium heat; add red pepper flakes and garlic, then cook 2 to 3 minutes. Add wine and reduce by half; turn off heat. In a bowl, add egg yolks and temper with pasta water, adding a little at a time and whisking constantly. Drain pasta (do not rinse) and reserve pasta water. Add pasta to skillet and toss to coat; stir in tempered egg yolks, cheeses and salt and pepper. Toss 2 to 3 more minutes, adding pasta water as needed if too dry. Garnish with parsley and enjoy.

Family Favorite

Strawberries Romanoff

This is a great light dessert to have after a heavy meal.

½ cup sour cream
3 tablespoons packed brown sugar
1 tablespoon brandy or cognac
(or vanilla extract)
½ cup heavy cream
3 tablespoons sugar
4 cups sliced fresh strawberries

In a bowl, mix together sour cream, brown sugar and brandy. In another bowl, whip cream with a handheld electric mixer until it begins to thicken; add sugar and whip until soft peaks form. Fold cream into sour cream mixture until blended. Layer a small glass dish with strawberries. Top with a layer of cream. Repeat layering once, then serve.

Restaurant Recipe

Mother Jug's Grill

523 South Mekusukey
Wewoka, OK 74884
405-257-9939
www.motherjugsgrill.com
Find us on Facebook

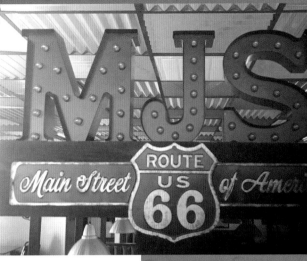

Owners Tonnya and Delbert Hisaw opened Mother Jug's Grill in March 2013. The name comes from an old Native American nickname of Delbert's from his youth: Jug, like a whiskey jug. Delbert is Pappa Jug, and Tonnya is the restaurant's namesake, Mother Jug. They initially served food out of a food truck and soon became famous for their home-style cooking. Shortly after becoming successful with their food truck, the couple decided to give the grill a permanent location. Mother Jug's is known for the names of the dishes served, which are oftentimes named after a local person or a Hisaw family member. Come experience Southern hospitality at its finest.

Monday – Wednesday: 6:30 am to 3:00 pm
Thursday & Friday: 6:30 am to 9:00 pm
Saturday: 6:30 am to 2:00 pm

Cowboy Tacos

1 (2-pound) bag pinto beans

1 (8.5-ounce) box Jiffy corn muffin mix
plus ingredients to prepare

2 pounds ground beef

Chopped onion, tomatoes and
lettuce for topping

Shredded cheese, salsa, sour cream and
jalapeños for topping

Soak beans in water in large bowl overnight; drain and rinse. Add beans to a large stockpot of water and cook at low boil 2 to 3½ hours or until beans are tender. Meanwhile, prepare Jiffy mix according to package instructions, baking in a 9x13-inch casserole dish; cool and cut into squares. In a large skillet, brown beef and drain fat. To serve, place a cornbread square on a plate and top with beans and beef. Top with remaining ingredients and enjoy.

Restaurant Recipe

RESTAURANT INDEX

RECIPE INDEX

C

MORE GREAT AMERICAN BOOKS

NEW

My Notebook Series

Alabama • Georgia • Mississippi

$14.95 • wire-o-bound • 5⅜ x 8¼ • 192 pages

NEW

Busy Moms: A Farm to Table
Fabulous Cookbook

$18.95 • 256 pages • 7x9
paperbound • full color

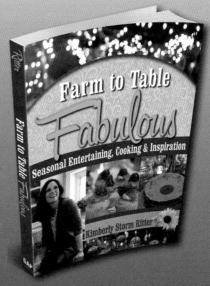

Farm to Table Fabulous

$18.95 • 256 pages • 7x9
paperbound • full color

Church Recipes are the Best

Georgia Church Suppers

$18.95 • 256 pages • 7x10 • paperbound • full color

Mississippi Church Suppers

$21.95 • 288 pages • 7x10 • paperbound • full color

Little Gulf Coast Seafood Cookbook

$14.95 • 192 pages • 5½x8½
paperbound • full color

Ultimate Venison Cookbook for Deer Camp

$21.95 • 288 pages • 7x10
paperbound • full color

Game for All Seasons Cookbook

$16.95 • 240 pages
7x10 • paperbound

Kids in the Kitchen
$18.95 • 256 pages
7x10 • paperbound • full color

Great American Grilling
$21.95 • 288 pages • 7x10
paperbound • full color

State Hometown Cookbook Series

A Hometown Taste of America, One State at a Time

EACH: $18.95 • 240 to 272 pages • 7x10 • paperbound • full color

**Alabama • Georgia • Louisiana • Mississippi
South Carolina • Tennessee • Texas • West Virginia**

Eat & Explore State Cookbook Series

Discover community celebrations and unique destinations, as they share their favorite recipes.

EACH: $18.95 • 256 pages • 7x9 • paperbound • full color

**Arkansas • Illinois • North Carolina
Ohio • Oklahoma • Virginia**

State Back Road Restaurant Recipes Cookbook Series

From two-lane highways and interstates to dirt roads and quaint downtowns, every road leads to delicious food when you're traveling across our United States. The STATE BACK ROAD RESTAURANT RECIPES COOKBOOK SERIES serves up a well-researched and charming guide to each state's best back road restaurants. No time to travel? No problem. Each restaurant shares with you their favorite recipes—sometimes their signature dish, sometimes a family favorite, but always delicious.

EACH: **$18.95** • **256 pages** • **7x9** • **paperbound** • **full color**

Alabama • Kentucky • Louisiana • Mississippi • Missouri
North Carolina • Oklahoma • South Carolina • Tennessee • Texas

3 Easy Ways to Order

1) Call toll-free **1-888-854-5954** to order by phone or to request a free catalog.

2) Order online at **www.GreatAmericanPublishers.com.**

3) Mail a check or money order for the cost of the book(s) plus $5 shipping for the first book and $1 for each additional plus a list of the books you want to order along with your name, address, phone, and email to:

Great American Publishers
171 Lone Pine Church Road
Lena, MS 39094

Find us on Facebook: www.facebook.com/GreatAmericanPublishers.

Join the **We Love 2 Cook Club** and get a 10% discount.
www.GreatAmericanPublishers.com

256